Sales Through Service

Transform your restaurant team into Sales and Service professionals

Joy Zarine & Deon van Niekerk

Copyright © 2020 The Hospitality Masters.

All rights reserved. No part of this book may be reproduced in any form on by an electronic or mechanical means, including information storage and retrieval systems, without permission in writing from the publisher, except by a reviewer who may quote brief passages in a review.

While the publisher and author have used their best efforts in preparing this book, they make no representations or warranties with respect to the accuracy or completeness of the contents of this document and specifically disclaim any implied warranties of merchantability or fitness for particular purpose. No warranty may be created or extended by sales representatives, promoters, or written sales materials.

The advice and strategies contained herein may not be suitable for your situation. Neither the publisher nor author shall be liable for any loss of profit or any other commercial damages, including but not limited to special, incidental, consequential, or other damages.

ISBN: 9798648582163

Dear reader,

We are so pleased you are here, welcome.

As this book was just about to go to print in early 2020, the global pandemic of Covid-19 spread across the planet, triggering a health and economic crisis we could never have imagined.

We wrestled with what to do with this book – as hundreds of thousands of restaurants were forced to close. Our industry (which for many was already a daily struggle) seemed to get unbelievably more challenging within a few days and a few government press conferences.

Contemplating the future from a "locked down" London in April 2020, it was impossible to know what to do with Sales Through Service, with no one to serve and no one to sell to. We reached out to a number of friends, clients and contacts across the hospitality industry and asked them all one simple question - does this book *still* matter? The response was unexpected and more than we could have ever imagined.

Everyone replied with a resounding "Yes!" With many more words of encouragement, we were told that the lessons from this book were important before this crisis and now they were essential to everyone who wants their business to survive in the future.

We, of course, don't have a crystal ball for what will happen next in the months and years to come. But one thing is certain. We don't want you, your restaurant and your team to just *survive* this crisis. We want you to *thrive*.

There will be many businesses unable to open again, and some owners unwilling to even try. On the flip side, there will be those that dare to dream that their restaurants will buzz with excitement and atmosphere, laughter and celebration once more. Life may not go back to exactly how it once was, but now is the time to take a step forward into your future. Your restaurant reimagined, with sales and service at the forefront.

Believe wholeheartedly that our world really needs what you offer. As a society, we want to be making memories with friends and family over fabulous food and drinks, and that will never go out of style.

So here it is – our book written and published for *you*.

You, who once had a dream, and who dares to keep going forward and building that dream, one plate, one glass and one guest at a time.

This book is and always will be, dedicated to you.

Deon & Joy

Contents

Preface by Deon	1
Preface by Joy	4
Sales: The Key to Unlocking Revenue in Your Business	7
The Importance of Sales	19
Creating a Sales Mindset	33
Developing Your Guest Journey	43
Management vs Leadership	66
The Service LAPS	76
What to Do When Things Go Wrong	101
The Smarter Way To Serve (and Sell)	115
Just Keep Growing	130
Time For Change? Time For Action	135
About the Authors	139

PREFACE BY DEON

The world is filled with advice on how to improve your business. There's the usual "get your staff to upsell", "encourage your guests to buy premium products", "give your guests bounce back vouchers". But rarely do you see a practical, comprehensive plan that you can easily implement which not only transforms your sales but, at the same time, increases your profit; and creates a business that supports the lifestyle you've truly desired.

Most sales in a restaurant are accidental; you sell a main course and a drink or whatever the guest happens to order. This is due to most front of house staff seeing themselves as being order takers.

One of the biggest challenges is that most waiting staff don't like selling. In fact, they loathe the idea of "having to sell". Knowing only too well how team members feel, we've developed a tried and tested approach that not only gets your staff over their fear or dislike of sales, but significantly increases your sales and profits.

I have worked in the hospitality sector my entire life. I studied marketing and sales management and have learned how to implement growth and revenue streams in restaurants.

Successful sales require engrained systems and processes, not just occasional activities, such as having haphazard upselling of expiring menu items. What works best is a system that your staff believes in and are comfortable to deliver which means they're in a better place to take ownership and deliver.

Proven to work best, is establishing a deliberate guest journey and a style of service that, surprisingly, doesn't feel like selling at all. Both of which are fundamental to achieving revenue targets. It's not about *thinking* outside the box but *selling* outside the box.

Sales Through Service is that system.

Our approach radically changes the way you view and treat your team and gives them the tools and knowledge to transform from being "order takers" to consummate "service and sales professionals".

This dramatically improves your business and ultimately, reduces staff turnover – a perennial problem that all hospitality owners face. This approach develops a culture where your employees take ownership and initiative way beyond their job descriptions.

Overnight success is a myth. Sales success requires some effort to implement but once embedded, the system virtually runs itself. Just like a plane needs maximum power to take off, but once airborne, it requires less power to stay up in the air.

Follow the guidance in the book and kick-start your higher, targeted sales by getting your staff to not only serve exceptionally but *sell* exceptionally.

Deon van Niekerk

PREFACE BY JOY

At the very beginning of my career in hospitality (as a waitress), I *hated* the idea of selling. Selling to me sounded pushy, false and completely against my moral code. If I was asked to sell something I would feel dread in the pit of my stomach – knowing it was going to end in embarrassment on my part, rejection from the recipient of my limp "sales pitch" and frustration from my boss with the lacklustre results (not a winning combination).

Salespeople in my mind were tacky fakers, dressed in ill-fitted shiny suits, pushing secondhand cars that were going to fall apart as soon as they rolled off the forecourt. But as time went on, my view of what it meant to sell and what it means to be a sales professional has really changed.

The truth is, I'm not a fake or a pushy person. But I am passionate about people and making others happy. I always wanted my guests to have a Five Star experience; I always wanted them to enjoy the best. If there was an incredible wine that would complement the steak, I wanted to tell my guests about it.

If there was a chef speciality that was worth talking about, there was no stopping me. If there was a way to enhance the experience for my guests... it was happening in my section. It was this passion that led to me becoming the top seller in the businesses I worked in and more often than not the top earner too.

With no falsities or pushy techniques, and hopefully no ill-fitting shiny suits either. Eventually I realised that sales is *never* about selling, it's really about the *service*. Today I label myself as "guest experience obsessed" and wear that title like a badge of honour. Often, I meet a restaurant teams who are the kindest, most pleasant people – yet they are lousy when it comes to selling.

The guests are left uninspired, and wanting more, with a good yet forgettable experience. The smiley staff take the orders, yet no one hears about the stunning Malbec or the award winning Black Cod, and both sit out back unsold.

When Deon and I created *Sales Through Service*, it was a meeting of the minds to stop the incessant order taking that was making business tougher than it needed to be and to create dynamic sales forces that transform the fortunes of restaurants across the globe.

Our training is changing the future for hundreds of front of house staff who are becoming sales professionals and enhancing the experience for the hundreds and thousands of guests who come into contact with these businesses.

We don't believe in complicated jargon and hours and hours of pointless ideas that would never really work in the "real world".

Sales and service are at the heart of everything we do and teach. Seeing what these changes mean to a business, their employees and their guests is everything to us. We are relentless about taking the fear out of selling and putting the passion back into your service, every single day.

Joy Zarine

SALES: THE KEY TO UNLOCKING REVENUE IN YOUR BUSINESS

There is no easy way to say this – your business could be in real trouble. The road ahead for you is destined to be incredibly bumpy, if your team are not service and sales professionals.

A few months ago, Deon and I had a meeting at a private members club in central London. Just a stone's throw away from the buzz of Trafalgar Square, every table was taken with busy businesspeople from the arts to the movies to who knows what! As we sat there discussing our plans for the next training sessions and conferences we would be attending, I looked around aghast at what I could see.

I counted upwards of around ten staff, from waiters to waitresses, bartenders and managers – all busy doing nothing. One was counting and wiping bottles, the other was emptying boxes, one was on the phone, another tapping away on their laptop. All busy doing little of value and *selling* nothing.

Despite the smiles of staff as they clear the empty glasses, if they're not selling, the tills won't fill themselves. We spoke to one of the managers and asked if they would ever be interested in training their team to serve and sell better.

Their response was one of frustration because he knew his team weren't great at sales but didn't really believe they could ever be. Then he said even if he wanted to try and train them, there was no money to do so.

We visited several times over the next few months and nothing changed. We would spend our money but only the bare minimum. There was never a better option offered, never an additional item suggested. We often felt like an inconvenience for wanting a refill.

As I looked around at all the tables, full of empty glasses, empty coffee cups, menus clutched with people wanting to order I realised – this business was never going to be here in years to come. How could it be? It was fascinating just how many people they would employ who did so little to help feed the business! Sales were so far away from being the priority.

Just as predicted, in January of this year an email hit my inbox from the Director of the members club stating it would not be opening again, blaming economic conditions and pressures of rent from the Landlord.

This person just didn't get it. Yes, there will always be an opportunity to blame someone, but the reality was he had a workforce of people reluctant to serve and unable to sell. As the Queen song goes...doof, doof, doof, another one bites the dust.

Now, imagine there was a magic formula that you could put into your business that increased your revenue and helped to ensure long term success. Furthermore, what if this magic formula wouldn't cost you anything other than a little effort to set up?

This magic formula would transform your personal earnings, your employees' earnings, enhance your guests' experiences and reviews, every time. You could actually enjoy some time off and appreciate your business more. Your staff turnover could be reduced and the consistency of service improved, imagine how that would feel?

We are not talking about revolutionising the way you do things, breaking down your business and starting from scratch. You already serve your guests and you are already making sales. We are talking about adding a few small steps into your service cycle that will *improve* the size of sales and give you incredible results as part of a deliberately designed guest experience.

Between us, we have nearly fifty years of hospitality experience (sad but true), and every day we see great businesses struggling because their staff don't know how to serve and, just as importantly, don't know how to sell.

We are contacted regularly by a wide variety of bar and restaurant owners needing our help.

Many are stressed out, feeling overworked and most are not achieving the financial results their businesses really deserve. When we meet with potential clients, we look at where they are with their business. For many of them, they are restaurant owners wanting to grow their business but struggling to make real profits.

General managers that are frustrated that their days are consumed with organising rotas, feeling trapped dealing with customer complaints, trying to motivate staff, and wearing hundreds of different hats in the business. Or even pub landlords stressing over spiralling taxes and costs, feeling tired of being stuck on this hamster wheel.

When meeting these owners and managers we ask them questions to find out more about what they want and need from us. What would make your days more enjoyable? How do you measure success in your restaurant? How would it feel to be more successful? How would it feel to have a thriving sales team, working front of house in your restaurant? What difference would more money and, more importantly, profits mean to your business, your life, and your future?

Most owners want financial consistency in their business and the confidence to take some time off. That's not how they describe it to us though. It's usually put to us in the form of staff recruitment and retention is difficult, Gen Z is not as committed as previous generations and that it all feels like really hard work.

Even the guests get accused of not wanting to spend any money and being unresponsive to staff. These owners often feel they cannot afford to take time away from their business in case something goes wrong and they need to oversee everything.

Almost all of them feel in their heart of hearts that the guest experience comes down to who served them, which staff were on duty and if the owner or manager was there or not.

Being profitable in the hospitality sector is tough. Day in and day out it's hard work and many owners feel they are stumbling from one crisis to the next. It's almost always the classic symptom of people working hard in their business and not concentrating *on* their business.

The simple solution is getting your guests to spend more and yes, we can easily achieve that. When we implement our system that changes a few small things and redirects the focus of the team, the results have been incredible. The magic formula comes into play and not only do the guests spend more, they *feel* happier.

In this book, we outline the principles of Sales Through Service and it's a great introduction to what we do and why we do it. The hospitality industry is challenging but we believe we can empower you and your team to become a passionate and driven sales machine that unlocks your business' potential.

We all need to learn to sell, but it's important to remember we are here to sell with purpose *and* professionalism. Following four steps, which we call the Service LAPS, is highly effective at improving sales whilst also improving the guest experience.

The Service LAPS is a process that you follow continuously throughout your shift. Like a Formula 1 driver, you keep doing the LAPS throughout your service, stopping for a pitstop if required of course! But everyone in the organisation needs to consider themselves part of the Service LAPS process, which in turn fits into each stage of your guest journey.

The Service LAPS works as follows:

Look at what your guests might need or want
Ask a relevant question
Propose a solution
Serve all guests well

Throughout this book we include real testimonials from people who have either completed one of our sales training development days or online training with The Hospitality Masters. We call these *Confessions of a Sales Pro*. If you feel you have sales pro success story to share once reading this book, please do let us know!

Email **hello@thehospitaliymasters.com**

Confessions of a Sales Pro

"As the owner of two restaurants, the idea of adding another expense really stressed me out. VAT returns, wages bills and spiralling supplier costs made my life a misery in the first three years of business. My business partner loved the idea of enrolling our staff into the Hospitality Masters and training them on how to sell at the table. I was beyond sceptical – but keen to be proven wrong, and I was! Within a month of the training, we could notice not only our sales going up but our spend per head and our reviews. Guests were happier that they were being served better products. I am kicking myself we didn't do it sooner. Sales Through Service has changed our business and reduced our stress levels."

For businesses that have used our Sales Through Service system, the results have been incredible. It's fair to say that bad service happens all by itself whilst good service needs to be measured, managed and improved in order to exist at all.

For guests, Sales Through Service upgrades their experience in restaurants from good to great. Delighting your guests through ideal recommendations and better service standards. You will see by having a deliberate guest journey, ensuring a positive experience, and introducing the Service LAPS (which only require small tweaks to what you are doing already) you'll gain massive net results.

To adopt this process, it's important to understand three main points:

- Your team needs an easy to follow system to guide them to a consistent, high-quality service.

- The reason so many people struggle to sell is because they don't believe in or understand what they're supposed to be selling.

- When it comes to selling to guests at the table, if you don't suggest it, they're not going to buy it! Your guests need to know what's on offer or they'll never know to order it.

This book has been written with the aim of giving you an immediate increase in sales, profits and service. Your guests will feel better looked after, your team members will receive better tips, better service charge and have a more enjoyable experience at work as well.

As a business owner, you'll feel less stress and more happiness. By creating small changes in your hospitality business, you can spark changes that unlock sales with ease. By following the steps outlined in this book, you can change the future for everyone involved in your business.

Sales through Service is not simply about transforming your team members into sales professionals but also developing your management team into a leadership team. It's about building solid structures in your business that not only improve your guests' experiences but also increase the overall value of your business.

If you run a restaurant in a major town or city like London, for example, you need to have something special to serve, something profitable to sell, and a team of energetic staff to sell those products. If you don't have these, there are around 39,999 other places for your guests to visit.

Restaurants without a Sales Through Service system can often feel like a struggle. Wages are a struggle to find, guests (and their complaints) are a struggle to deal with, suppliers' invoices are eye-watering and don't get me started on those never-ending utility bills!

Too often it's people passionate about food or drinks and customer service who start restaurants – the business acumen and grasp on the numbers is an afterthought that many believe will just fall into place. Unfortunately, it doesn't. Once the shine fades off a new business, there must be some real systems in place to drive people back time and time again, otherwise guests will just keep heading to the next new shiny spot on the high street.

POINTS TO CONSIDER

- What makes your restaurant different?
- What experiences are you capable of delivering well and consistently?
- What are you known for?
- What are the key stages of your customer journey?

- What are the emotional responses you are hoping to elicit from your guests?
- What can often go wrong in the restaurant? (Look at your online reviews and speak to staff and guests).
- What actions do you expect your staff to take when things go wrong?
- What system do you use (if any) to record or measure your sales success?

Deon and I are both hypersensitive when it comes to hospitality businesses – it's hard to turn those "spidey-senses" off. We can't help but want places to just get it right or at least be aware of when they get it wrong. We want to help business owners develop their teams to be better. After all, when they're skilled at service and sales, everyone wins!

We have trained people individually and together for many years and everything we teach holds the guest at the front and centre. Eventually, we wanted to put our ideas and systems down on paper, which led to this book, an online sales training academy and our live development days. What we teach doesn't have to cause huge changes or huge revolution in your business.

Often, it is small steps in the right direction every day that evolve the business from *surviving* to *thriving*. If you embrace our concepts and decide to make the change in your business to adopt the Sales through Service way, the future is bright and profitable!

Understand that even small changes within your business can have a huge impact on the profits. A £5 increase on your spend per head should be very achievable.

Imagine the sale of an extra side, a second glass of wine or even just a simple dessert.

But look what it does when multiplied by every single one of your guests:

If you serve 100 guests per day this can add and additional £500 of top-line sales every day

= An additional £182,000 per year

If you serve 200 guests per year

= An additional £364,000 per year.

Wow. What a difference a sale makes!

RESOURCES AVAILABLE TO HELP YOU SUCCEED

We know how busy you are, so our aim is to keep this book short and valuable to improve sales within your business. There are references throughout for downloads that are available on our website – The Hospitality Masters. We also hold a number of live events and have a busy online community that expands on our techniques and training which you can also find on our website. www.thehospitalitymasters.com

By the end of this book, you will clearly understand how to implement the two important steps of the Sales Through Service system that your business needs to succeed: The Deliberate Guest Journey and how to do The Service LAPS.

If you are interested in taking the next steps with us for yourself or team members, our online Sales Through Service Programme is available online at a reasonable cost – a fraction of what you stand to earn by implementing the programme. It's easy to action and will transform your team's performance and your business.

We also offer in-house consultancy along with a range of tools available to help you and your team succeed. We would love to hear from you so get in touch via our website **www.thehospitalitymasters.com**

Ready to serve better and to sell more? Let's get started.

THE IMPORTANCE OF SALES

Whenever reports of a national restaurant heading into administration hit the news, with spiralling debt and thousands of jobs under threat, the airwaves are awash with umpteen reasons why the business failed.

From greedy landlords to rising business rates, political interference, politicians' apathy, staff shortages or the rise in veganism – the excuses go on and on. But there is only *one* reason why a restaurant business fails, and that is they do not make *enough* sales.

Of course, you have to manage expenses and cash flow, but sales are to businesses what oxygen is to us humans. Without enough sales, your business will eventually suffocate and die.

Sales are your company's essential ingredient for survival. All the press coverage, industry awards and smiley staff won't pay the bills if your tills aren't ringing. Ultimately, there are two outcomes, either you make a profit or you perish.

Unfortunately, in our industry, you cannot rely on the greatest salespeople walking through the door and asking for a job.

Those people are already working for companies like Rolex, Tesla and Google.

Successful companies like these not only have superior (and often revolutionary) products they also have exceptional sales forces. But of more relevance to you is that these companies and thousands of others like them have comprehensive training programmes in place for their staff (FYI, they're not counting on the greatest salespeople walking through doors either!).

Rolex has a training centre in Geneva dedicated to talent and employee development. It provides continuing education for the company's employees and managers and instruction for apprentices with the aim of ensuring the future of the workforce in line with the brand's values.

That aim is explained to staff as "Product Culture" which transmits knowledge about Rolex watches and heritage. Ultimately, the vision is clear – they want to make more sales. The company policy states that *everyone* who works for Rolex has a sales role.

Isn't that the same in your business? Aren't we *all* in sales in some way? Like Rolex, sales need to be at the focus for all your staff. It doesn't matter about job titles or which department they work in – everyone is in sales.

Most restaurants, however, don't have any formal sales training programme in place. Even more concerning is that there is no particular focus put on sales training.

Restaurant sales are registered through the tills and staff are encouraged to upsell but in terms of measuring results and implementing a formal system to use, well, that rarely happens.

Whilst you may feel you don't have the greatest salespeople walking through your door, that doesn't matter. All Rolex actually has is a systematic and consistent approach to its customers and their customer experience. You can have the exact same approach and build and nurture your own Rolex-caliber team. And it's easier than you think.

All you need to do is develop your own guest journey and experience and build a team of sales professionals rather than have a haphazard guest experience and a team of smiley and well-mannered order takers. Like Rolex, sales need to be front and centre of your team's focus. It doesn't matter about job titles – from head chef to busboy, everyone is in sales!

THE VICIOUS CYCLE OF SERVICE TODAY

Restaurateurs often think of themselves in the food, beverage or hospitality business. The truth is, we're in the business of making memories, making sales, great guest experiences and winning *repeat* business. If we overlook the opportunity to win a guest once and build a relationship of loyalty with them, the business is far tougher to grow.

Too often, bars and restaurants are caught in a vicious cycle of trying to survive by spending huge amounts of money on marketing to constantly attract *new* guests through the door. To try and win guests over from the competition they end up adding discount deals, happy hours, 2-4-1 meal deals, bottomless brunch, etc.

At the same time, they have a huge in-house focus on cutting costs by trimming down staff numbers and wages, cutting portions sizes, demanding staff carry out menial duties, attempting to be efficient and financially savvy.

Of course, guests don't appreciate these cost-cutting measures! Our guests care about their experience, our hospitality, and how we make them feel.

Hospitality is the warm welcome and the fond farewell, a genuine smile, a caring attitude and the personal attention your business gives your guests.

It's the recommendations your team make and the interest you show in the guests regarding their likes and dislikes. Being hospitable is an *emotional* skill – how you make someone feel. Good hospitality improves the ability of staff to personally connect with guests and is the most important element in the guest experience.

A poor in-store experience lowers the chance of repeat business and results in online reviews being average or poor.

The restaurant then has to spend money on trying to encourage guests to return by offering endless loyalty schemes and bounce-back offers.

Staff end up overworked, guests are underwhelmed, and managers are stressed and under pressure.

There is no point in being able to clear plates, spin bottles, shake cocktails and pour wine technically well if you do it with awkwardness, arrogance or in an unfriendly manner.

Your guests are on an *emotional* journey throughout their visit to your restaurant and this ends up being either positive or negative. As business owners, we need to ensure all our staff are aware of the guest journey and the touchpoints for each stage to ensure it's a positive experience.

Sales Through Service facilitates this positive experience but only works well if you have built trust and rapport with your guests from the outset of their visit. We need to be aware of the opportunities to sell and to serve and maximise sales when it is right to do so. Embracing opportunities to sell is the ultimate game-changer for your business.

ORDER TAKERS VS SALES PROFESSIONALS

Imagine being shown around a new apartment by an estate agent.

You are shown through the front door and allowed to walk around the apartment without your agent saying a word.

From what you can see it all looks in good order, however, some of the doors are locked shut and some of the window shutters bolted closed. By the end of the limited and basic tour you are presented with an offer sheet – what offer would you like to make?

In contrast, imagine being shown around the same apartment by a knowledgeable, passionate and professional agent. Not only do they take their time to show you around every corner of the apartment but they also unlock all the doors and tell you about all the modern additions that have been made.

Beyond that, the agent enquires whether you are a passionate and enthusiastic cook. You are? Wonderful! You are shown the impressive oven and stove along with the extraction fan and beautiful views from the kitchen windows.

Is security a concern for you?
There are secure locks on all doors and windows, the entrance is covered by CCTV and there is even a camera that connects to your smartphone so you can keep an eye on your property from wherever you are in the world.

Do you have young children?

The surrounding towns, school OFSTED reports and various transport links are all explained in detail and all of your questions and concerns are covered. Finally, an offer sheet is presented to you – how much higher would your offer be now?

Same apartment but the sales *professional* will be receiving the highest offer every single time.

Too often a similar experience is being offered to guests in restaurants. Menus go unexplained, signature dishes go unmentioned and the role of the staff is one of an order taker, rather than a sales professional.

The order taker can be defined as a team member who takes the orders of food and drinks but doesn't make any attempts to increase existing sales, increase the frequency of orders or help turn guests into repeat visitors.

They are not unfriendly but do little to enhance your reputation and tend to get by on minimal efforts. Their spend per head is average and the average is definitely much lower than it should be. If they were estate agents, they'd be leaving the doors locked on their house visit and just hoping for the best.

In contrast, the sales professional is the team member who actively recommends items off the menu to suit the guest, delivers you a great spend per head and leaves the guest feeling good about themselves and your business. They take advantage of sales opportunities that present themselves.

Providing your guests with good service is a base expectation of your team's job but good service by itself does not necessarily translate into good sales.

A good example of good service resulting in poor sales is a scenario that is played out on restaurants across the globe...

The guests have finished eating their main courses and the waiter clears the table efficiently. They then present the dessert menus to them saying something along the lines of how great your desserts are. Whilst this is an example of good service, it's likely to result in poor sales.

The guests haven't been inspired to order a particular dessert; they haven't felt compelled to really want to try something. In order to get the desserts order, the guest should gain a recommendation that sparks a desire to really want to try it. By creating a mental picture for the guest, they'll hopefully be salivating at the thought!

For your staff to sell successfully, they need to understand the sales process. This is what the Service LAPS is all about. It's not about telling your team once and hoping they get it. It's about training them with the system and guiding them again and again on how to do it better and be more successful.

The sales process needs to happen within a well thought out guest journey. When serving your guests, your front of house team should constantly be doing the Service LAPS (which we'll cover later).

WHY YOUR STAFF (REALLY) HATE TO SELL

Before we dive into the "how" of selling through service, there is an important barrier that needs to be overcome. Something that you no doubt know already!

It's human nature for most of us to be uncomfortable selling anything. Many of your staff will detest the very notion of sales since it just doesn't come naturally at all.

So what is it about selling that makes people in all industries run for the hills? Why do people often feel so awkward or uncomfortable by the very thought of upselling or suggestive selling, especially in a restaurant environment?

Having worked with thousands of hospitality staff over the years, we have noticed five main reasons so many feel reluctant to sell:

- They feel that selling feels false, pushy or misleading.

- They lack confidence and are scared the guest will say no and they will feel rejected or embarrassed.

- They are not sure how to approach making proactive sales.

- They have poor product knowledge, or they don't believe in or understand the product.

- There is no formal recognition or rewards in place for any extra effort.

Front of house staff want to (rightly) come across as being genuine to their guests and don't want to do anything that feels fake or pushy. Whilst comfortable in serving guests, selling to them can feel scary. The underlying issue is often a lack of product knowledge and confidence, and a lack of incentives mean there isn't a positive environment that encourages sales success.

Of course, there is another reason that prevents someone from becoming a sales professional, and that's a poor attitude. This is something that's very tough to change, don't kid yourself. Once a sales system is in place, you need to have the right staff with the right attitude, otherwise the struggles will continue (I know we mentioned the magic formula at the beginning of this book, but just to be clear, we're not magicians!).

Whilst most of your staff want to provide good service and most likely do, the problem is obvious.

If all your staff only *serve well* and never sell, you could be in hot water. You cannot afford to only sell by accident. Accidental sales are things such as main courses and the first beverage. Your team needs to sell *with purpose* and professionalism in order to serve and sell well.

Having worked in the industry our entire working lives we know that for staff to sell successfully it has to feel natural. It has to be part of a process that fits seamlessly into serving guests and not feel fake, fraudulent or forced.

No one wants to feel like a sleazy salesman, tricking your way to the top. Sales professionals need to have clear guidelines and steps and know what they are selling. The process should be an intrinsic part of the guest experience and delivered consistently every single time.

We are very fortunate in our industry that the people who step inside our businesses have seriously come to buy. Unlike a shoe shop or fashion boutique where customers are there to browse, restaurant guests are hungry and ready to order (and spend).

Our guests are committed buyers, yet staff can feel uncomfortable at the thought of *selling* them something.

So, it's our job to show them how to sell confidently, how to serve efficiently and create a guest experience that people cannot help but love.

When your team understands the importance of the guest journey and how the Service LAPS fits seamlessly into it, they will realise that the guests are there to buy and appreciate guidance.

By following our process, they will not be made to feel embarrassed or rejected and will be delivering exceptional, effective service at all times. They will build rapport with their guests and feel relaxed. If not, you will have a team full of order takers and let's be honest, can your business really afford that?

QUICK STEPS TO SUCCESS

Remember that we're all in Sales. So often we come across staff that don't see the broader picture of their role and are narrowly focused on their specific job.

Ultimately, it's everyone's job to ensure the business is as profitable and successful as possible. Everyone forms part of the guest journey and has a direct influence on whether it's a positive one. You are more likely to succeed if your team are all on the same page.

Speak the same language

Ensure that all your staff use the same terminology for the various activities undertaken. For example, ensure that chefs are part of the process in deciding how to describe dishes.

No one knows more about the ingredients, preparation and flavours of your dishes than your talented and hard-working chefs. Put them front and centre of your pre-service meetings every single day.

They are the key to unlocking vast amounts of knowledge in your team. When it comes to the language you all use, talk about *guests*, not customers; talk about *services*, not shifts. The language you use in the business is vital when setting the tone and everyone needs to be on the same page.

Give feedback to all

Involve all your team members in successes and feedback – not just your front of house team. Reward support staff for success and acknowledge their contribution. No one gives a five-star review when their plate was dirty or their chips were cold; everyone plays their part in a story of success.

Set team targets

Goals, targets and objectives need to be shared and reinforced at pre-service meetings, team meetings, on notice boards and progress continually fed back to all. Knowledge is power in your business – progress reports and experience analysis are important to discuss the actual results versus desired ones.

Involve team members when setting targets. What is a realistic spend per head to aim for? How quickly can you turn the tables? How quickly should drinks be delivered once ordered? Likewise, with the delivery of food – consider both speed and presentation. Agree upon the standards with their involvement and they will be more achievable and acted upon.

A strong team culture in any company should focus on creating an environment where the whole team has a sales role and sees themselves as sales and service professionals.

There are effectively only two roles in any hospitality business:

- **The staff involved in direct sales**

- **The rest of the staff who are in a sales support role**

Our training system helps to develop teams of confident and knowledgeable sales professionals, whatever their role. The best part is, the system is designed to not even feel like selling – just providing great customer service that gets positive results for the server, the guests and for your business.

CREATING A SALES MINDSET

Before we get into the system of making more sales by delivering better service, it's important to understand the impact of mindset when it comes to being a sales professional.

We understand why you, the business owner or manager, wants your team to sell more – it sure is tough at the top when you're drowning in bills. But when we train hospitality teams, one of the toughest challenges we tackle first is how to help them adopt a sales mindset and empower them as a team to become a sales force. Make no mistake, this is what you and your business need them to be.

It is not (and cannot be) your job as the manager to serve every guest, check on every table, explain every special and present everyone with the bill promptly. However, it is your job to give your team the tools and training they need to succeed in their position.

Successful sales teams have well-defined systems to help them grow, learn and achieve. You need to have some way of delivering on-going advanced sales training for your entire team and know how you are going to implement that training programme.

You also need to understand that to many (if not all) of your workforce, a £100 bottle of wine seems ridiculous – actually beyond ridiculous, it seems foolish! But to the semi-retired property mogul, it represents everything he wants to show his loved ones. Luxury, reward, indulgence and, let's face it, incredible wine!

To him, the price tag comes with the territory. Let's be honest, if the identical wine had a £9.99 label on it, he wouldn't even want it. So our duty to him is to not only serve it but to do our part in *selling* it to him.

Let's look at another example that your team may understand a little more easily. Imagine you're the world's biggest Beyoncé fan (not too tough to do I'm sure). Beyoncé's concert tickets are announced and you sit online poised to make your purchase. When you go to click and buy the tickets, you hover over two options – "best seats available" or "cheapest seats available".

Deals pop up offering suite packages, pre-show dining packages, champagne packages, and it's time to make your decision. Do you opt for the two cheap seats in the nosebleed section? Of course not. As the world's biggest Beyoncé fan, you're excited to go all out.

When it comes to the first date, the birthday celebration, the anniversary meal or the catch up between friends – we are here to provide guests with the most fulfilling and exceptional experience we can.

When we only take their orders, we are showing them straight to the nosebleed section. How do those fans feel watching Beyoncé as a little dot a mile away? Not great I imagine.

This is what Sales Through Service is all about. It's empowering your team with the confidence to deliver the highest possible service by recommending the best options available.

Confessions of a Sales Pro

"I just could not get my head around why people would ever want to even be offered a bottle of wine that costs as much as one week's rent! I am studying at University and waiting tables a few nights a week to help pay my bills (and give me a bit of beer money for the student union one night a week). Money was scarce and I was always so worried about not wasting any of it! My mind would be blown when people would opt away from my standard options of house wine and go for expensive champagne! Why would anyone want to set fire to their cash like that?

Then I encountered Sales Through Service and I realised I was putting my own preconceptions around cash onto everyone else and muddying what I was there to do – give my guests the best night possible! Although I am a (somewhat poor) student, this will not be my financial reality forever. I am studying hard to one day have a high paying job and when that happens, maybe I will want to enjoy the fruits of my success and enjoy the finer things in life.

Now I understand it's not about the value I put on a meal, it's the value and service I can offer my guests. I now spend my time gladly recommending the best options my restaurant has to offer. My guests love it and I'm so happy to say the better tips have meant I work one less shift per week and have more time to study (and visit the student union)."

Ambassadors vs Assassins

There are two types of people working in your business – ambassadors and assassins. Ambassadors are the employees who speak positively about your business whether they are on shift or not.

They adopt the company values as their own and pull together with their team members whenever the pressure is on. If there was a piece of rubbish on the restaurant floor, they wouldn't walk past it and ignore it, they would see it as their duty to pick it up.

The alternative is Assassins. These are negative about change, negative about new systems and work more for their own gain rather than for the greater good. Bad attitudes, low work ethic and people who undermine leadership are assassins in your business.

Everyone can sit through a training session and be taught how to do things in a new way. However, there needs to be a willingness to follow a new way and develop their skills.

The longer you let Assassins stay around, the more it's costing you and the more they are infecting those around them. Too often we have seen these terrible staff members survive in their jobs as they are seen as a pair of hands that is better than no pair of hands. Challenge the status quo and put your business and overall team first. Don't let one person derail your success, let them go. It will force you into filling the gap with an Ambassador for your business.

QUICK STEPS TO SUCCESS

Create a sales environment

Just like the old adage *"Good service needs to be managed – bad service happens all by itself"*, transforming your team from order takers to sales professionals doesn't happen by itself or by luck – it needs to be carefully managed.

The culture within your business reflects what you stand for, what you value and what you aspire to achieve. It defines your company's personality and shapes how you behave, work and communicate.

Sometimes companies try to grow sales by simply putting more pressure on the team – telling them to push premium products and upsell, simply trying to sell endless bottles of bubbly!

This is well intentioned, but ultimately doomed to failure and results in high staff turnover and guests feeling taken advantage of. Often it is potluck whether something premium or highly profitable is sold, and the business is trudging along on accidental sales.
Set clear goals and expectations

Clear communication about targets and expectations is a must. Targets should be challenging enough to keep your team engaged, but also achievable. These targets also need to be in line with your guest demographic and market positioning.

You don't want to create a situation where guests suffer from bill shock and feel ripped off. Targets and goals should be realistic, achievable and still offer value for money for the guests. You also need to clearly demonstrate how these targets can be achieved and what sales it would take to hit them.

Reward, reward, reward

Yes, it's so important that I'll say it again (and again). Recognition and rewards are essential for building up (and keeping) your sales force. It's worth noting when staff hit their targets but it's also important to recognise other things as well.

You might recognise a team member who deals with customer complaints well, or someone achieving great Tripadvisor reviews. Most employees want to feel their contribution *really* matters.

Your entire team is integral to a culture of success, so be proactive about giving them the respect and appreciation they deserve.

When I worked at The Ivy, the first people I was introduced to were the kitchen porters. They were described as the key team members. A small example, but endemic of how they created a service and sales culture throughout the company, across all departments.

Ignite passion

Share your company's long-term goals with your team. Give them something to believe in and strive for. Successes often comes down to openness, communication and above all, trust. Your team must understand there is a bigger goal behind every sale and that their contribution really matters.

As the manager, you need to keep your team passionate and excited about what they are selling. Tasting sessions and pre-service meetings both play a part in keeping your team inspired and enthusiastic on a daily basis.

Encourage learning and development

Don't let your "spend per head" monopolise your goals. Whilst it is a great measuring stick to grow your sales, also consider setting other targets to enhance a team member's skills.

For example, we have created a series of informative guides to share with staff on wines, spirits, beers and food. Or get your suppliers in to do tastings or visit their factories or farms.

Your employees need to feel valued and they will appreciate your willingness to invest in their ongoing learning and development. By demonstrating your dedication to their growth professionally, financially and personally, you will see increased productivity.
Drive activity as much as results

Sales are and always will be a numbers game. Often, however, some sections and tables are better than others and more conducive to sales. Some guests will not spend as much money as other guests regardless of what you do or offer. You may have a slow day due to inclement weather or where you are in the payday cycle.

Your teams have little control over these events and situations, so it's important to drive the sales process and the positive guest journey at all times. Whilst results are important, it's crucial to remember that if the correct process is in place and carried out each time, results will follow.

Build a strong team ethic

Your team should understand the company won't hit its revenue targets if only one or two servers perform well. So, you need to put processes in place to facilitate knowledge sharing.

Schedule team meetings to share success stories and challenges. Appoint specific employees as subject-matter experts to capitalise on individual strengths. Ask the head chef or sous chef to present on some dishes, or your bartenders to run a cocktail tasting.

It's also important to foster a positive team spirit that whilst competitive, is not overly so. Make time for team-building activities, nights out and occasional staff parties.

Selling outside the box

You've heard of thinking outside the box, well, the key to good sales in your business is *selling* outside the box.

Your guests have come in to buy – their buying decision was made as they stepped inside the front door. So now what? The fact that they are going to buy is undisputed. But what they buy and how much of it, well, that is to be decided.

Let's consider for a moment that you could score points based on what your guests were going to buy. But there are no points for main courses or first drinks.

All the points to be scored happen outside the box – your job (or your team members' job) is to get selling outside the box. We'll dive into how we do this later, but just let that vital point sink in – there are no points for mains or the first drink. Everything else? Well, the points are all to play for!

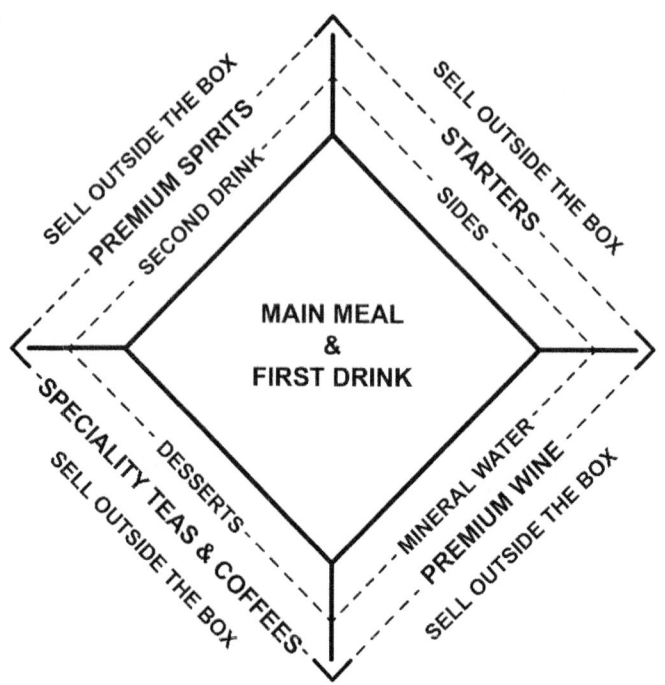

SELLING OUTSIDE THE BOX

DEVELOPING YOUR GUEST JOURNEY

If you really want to see results from Sales Through Service, you must map out a guest journey for your business. Once your team understands how using the Service LAPS fits into a positive guest journey, they will feel more confident and able to make positive sales suggestions.

Ultimately, guests want to order (and buy) items from people they feel they know, like and trust. If guests enjoy their time with you and the guest experience is positive, they will spend more money during their visit, return as a repeat guest and spread positive words about your restaurant.

Conversely, a negative experience will result in them tightening their wallets, not wanting to return and spreading negative word of mouth and reviews.

Lots of restaurants that we speak to seem to have a general understanding of their guest journey but most leave it to chance. It falls into a category of art rather than science! More often than not, the owners and managers have some solid ideas of what they *think* happens, the front of house team less so and the back of house team very little, if any at all.

If your team members don't know what is supposed to be happening with your guests at each step of the way, they'll have a tough time trying to get it right consistently.

It needs to be well thought out, shared and must become part of the culture in your restaurant.

The guest journey is made up of three parts:

Concept – *the style of your restaurant.* This will dictate the type of food, drinks and service offered, the music played, the atmosphere and tempo of service.

Execution – *the actual delivery of service.* It includes the physical skills you have including how you open a bottle of wine, how you carry plates, how you clear a table. It's also how long the food and drinks take to arrive and how it looks and is presented.

Hospitality – *the way you make people feel.* This is the important part that ends up separating the amateurs from the professionals. It is the warm, genuine welcome, the fond farewell, and all of the emotional interactions in between.

It is essential to remember that how we make our guests *feel* is ultimately going to determine the success or failure of our sales efforts, along with the fortune of the establishment. We should always aim to give a positive guest experience and elicit positive emotions from them.

By following some of our tips, you will discover ways to leave your guests feeling not only very satisfied and impressed but also emotionally connected to your restaurant and very likely to return.

Knowledgeable servers

One of the most important aspects of the guest experience is having team members who are well versed in your restaurant, its surrounding areas and, of course, your menu.

This means being able to suggest items based on your guest's preferences, wine pairings for certain dishes, being able to describe ingredients and say how the meal is prepared (roasted, grilled, fried, etc.), as well as knowing about the preparation time of dishes. It's also exceptional when you can guide your guests onto their next destination or know the curtain calls for the theatre around the corner.

Having excellent knowledge creates an amazing environment for your guests and gives them a fantastic experience by ensuring they have all the information they need and are guided throughout their meal.
Menu flexibility

It's important for your team to understand what can and cannot be changed with dishes. For example, what can be made vegetarian, vegan, or gluten-free? Within reason, you need to be able to offer a degree of flexibility with your menu items if guests ask for the removal or substitution of certain ingredients. It can be frustrating for guests if simple changes cannot be made so it's important that your servers know what's feasible for the kitchen.

Managing your guests' expectations

Sometimes things don't go according to plan. Certain dishes take longer to prepare and sometimes your kitchen and bar are just slammed.

By keeping guests informed of likely waiting times for tables, drinks, food and being upfront about the problem, most guests will give you the time you need to resolve it without writing a bad review afterwards. When people are left in the dark, frustrations can escalate quickly.

Sometimes guests can have slightly unrealistic ideas of how fast the drinks and food will appear or how quickly they should get a table. If someone orders a well-done steak, they need to be informed it may take 25 minutes. In this case, they might want to order something else if they are in a rush.

Mapping the guest journey

Understand what the guest journey is in your restaurant, the emotions that go alongside that journey, and what a positive and negative experience looks (and feels) like for the guest.

Like accidental sales that are inconsistent, an accidental guest journey results in inconsistent guest experiences.

We need to work on the areas that are in most need of improvement first. Eventually, you want to ensure the time your guests spend in your business is effortlessly exceptional, and your entire team consistently executes this journey, every single time.

If you're unsure about what areas need improving specifically, take a good look at your reviews. There should be plenty of clues there for where there is room to improve!

Of course, all restaurants are very different but in basic terms, we have identified five key stages that your guests will typically go through:

1) The Approach
2) The Greeting (meeting and seating)
3) The Order and Delivery (of food and drinks)
4) The Payment
5) The Departure

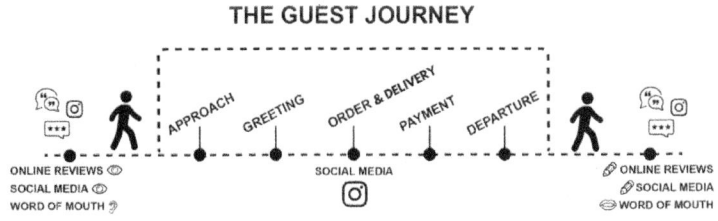

The experience we deliver to our guests at each of these stages goes towards how they will *feel* by the end of their journey with us. Although they may not realise it, with every interaction and at every stage, our guests are judging whether they have made a good decision choosing us and, more importantly, if they want to visit us (and recommend us) in the future.

There are endless opportunities for us to exceed our guests' expectations and deliver an exceptional experience, however, there are equal opportunities for it all to go wrong! Before even walking up to the restaurant the guests have probably done some research either online looking at reviews, social media or menus or perhaps have been recommended via word of mouth.

Likewise, once they leave they will go out into the world and tell others how their experience was. This means every stage of the experience can have consequences (either positive or negative) for your business.

Let's walk through a typical guest journey in a local restaurant through the eyes of the guests.

STEP 1: THE APPROACH

This is where curb appeal counts! As managers and employees, we breeze in through the front door or the side entrance and take little notice of what is right under our noses.

But we need fresh eyes on the prize when it comes to the approach. We need to see what our guests will see and make sure we are giving people the best possible start to their journey with us.

A Negative Experience

My family and I are walking up to the front of the restaurant to celebrate my sister's birthday. We've heard a lot of good things about this place, but the outside looks a little grubby. The ground is littered with cigarette butts, the sign lights are off and the menu is missing from the display cabinet. Not too sure this is going to be a great experience. If they don't clean the front of their restaurant, what else don't they clean? Feeling slightly nervous, wary and anxious.

A Positive Experience

My family and I are walking up to the front of the restaurant to celebrate my sister's birthday. We have heard a lot of good things about this place, the signage looks attractive and well-lit, windows look clean, the menu at the front looks interesting, the seats outside look clean, cosy and inviting. We're feeling excited, slightly nervous and optimistic!

SALES PRO TIPS

Get set for success

Your pre-service meetings should not just be about products and bookings. Take a look around – what does the front entrance look like? Is it clear of litter, cigarette butts and are the signage, doors and windows clean? Your curb appeal matters so make sure standards are kept high.

Steady that table

Wobbles happen to the best of us, not least our tables! Tables should always be checked pre-service so they are level without anyone having to ask. Fix it before guests are seated – no one enjoys a wobbly table or chair and if a wobbly table results in a glass of wine toppling over onto someone – it could ruin someone's evening with you. Steady that table!

First impressions count

Always offer a warm welcome and smile to anyone entering your restaurant or section. Our businesses thrive when guests feel happy and content when visiting us, and smiles are contagious so keep smiling!

STEP 2: THE GREETING

We should never underestimate how tentative people can be when entering our restaurants. They've often heard good things, but this is the point where the rubber hits the road – it's our time to shine and where the first impressions of our team really count.

A Negative Experience

We walk through the front door and stand waiting to be seated for a few minutes. The staff members appear to see us but ignore us. We are left standing there wondering what is going on – have we come to the right place? Do we need to seat ourselves? Should we go and find somewhere else to go? Eventually, someone comes over and takes our name. They find our reservation, but the tables haven't been organised and put together yet so we stand and wait as they hurriedly drag a few tables together. We can't help but feel concerned, frustrated, anticipation and stressed.

A Positive Experience

We walk through the front door and receive a warm and genuine welcome. We're shown to our table, which has already been set up for us as one long party-style table. Every setting has cutlery, wine glasses and menus. We feel like this is a great place to be, with a lovely greeting, we feel excited about what's next. We are feeling relaxed, content, and happy with everything so far.

SALES PRO TIPS

Minimise interruption

Try and wait for the right moment to approach the guests. It can be tricky but try not to barge into people's conversations or greetings. Their experience is about them, not about you! Just take a moment. Let the guest feel your presence at the table before you start talking.

Nothing is a problem

When someone has special requirements for food, drinks, seating arrangements, etc., always reassure them you'll do everything you can to try and meet their needs. If you can, substitute one vegetable or topping for another – don't make dramas or episodes unnecessarily. Don't just meet their expectations really try to exceed them.

Knowledge is power

In order to be a sales professional, you must know your menu inside and out and know which drinks to pair with which dishes.

Have great recommendations for different occasions and types of guests, and always let your guests know if something is sold out or unavailable before they read the menu and try to order the missing dish. Beyond this - having knowledge about your guests is also powerful.

Enquire how their day has been; if they are here to celebrate something special tonight, do they have any plans for the rest of the evening? By finding out if they are planning to be with you for 45 minutes or 3 hours you can adapt your service and your subsequent sales to accommodate them. If they are in a rush let your kitchen team know, and if they are not get ready with some incredible wine, cocktail or dessert recommendations. Remember to sell outside the box!

Allergy advice

Find out if anyone has any allergies. This isn't a maybe anymore – this is an essential part of service today. It really is a matter of life and death for some people. Be confident of where you can find the allergen information and always double-check, never guess.

STEP 3: THE ORDER AND DELIVERY OF FOOD AND DRINKS

During this part of the guest journey, we have the opportunity to prove we are professionals, not amateurs. It's not just about being friendly; it's about being knowledgeable and professional.

This is where the Service LAPS can be used time and time again: we look at whom we are serving; we ask a relevant golden question; we propose a great suggestion with their answers in mind, and go above and beyond with the service.

A Negative Experience

The waiter hurriedly offers us menus before telling us we need to be off the table before 9pm and then forgot all about us. Eventually, after 20 minutes he returns to take orders, then reveals two of the dishes we wanted to order were sold out. When the food comes, only half the items are brought to the table, everyone sits and waits for the remaining dishes, which are another five minutes. They are then brought out with no apology or explanation. We sat there thinking, "What is going on here? Aren't we supposed to be the customer and really feel looked after?" We feel like we are an inconvenience – I can't believe how badly we are being treated when all we want is dinner and a few drinks! We feel frustrated, angry, disappointed.

A Positive Experience

The waiter spots the balloons we have brought with us and asks about the occasion we are celebrating, wishing our family member a very happy 21st birthday. They recommend tonight's specials and what wines will go with each of our courses. The birthday girl is presented with a special celebration cocktail to mark the event.

Off the back of her delight, we all decide to join her and order our own cocktails! Every item was brought to the table together except for one side of garlic bread. As soon as it was remembered the server added it to the table, apologising for the delay. We are always being attended to – when drinks are nearly finished, we hear more recommendations. More drinks and more delicious cocktails follow!

At the end of the meal, a small birthday cake is brought out to mark the occasion. We feel really well taken care of and the meal feels like a true birthday celebration.

The food has been served promptly and is delicious! We love the cocktails and the tailored recommendations we have received. We have tried so many things we wouldn't usually order. What a great place! We feel joy, satisfaction, surprise, delight and awe!

SALES PRO TIPS

Look me in the eye

Where possible, turn to face the person ordering, try and position yourself at a part of the table where everyone can see you. Do not stand behind someone who is ordering and do your best to make eye contact. Thank him or her and repeat the order back to them.
It's not about you

Make the experience in your restaurant all about your guests' likes and dislikes. Be respectful of others for their choices; food is a very personal choice so be understanding of everyone. It's important to not to discuss your own eating habits and imply them onto others, be you vegetarian, vegan or fruitarian!

Advise wisely

Always give your guests the right guidance when ordering – you don't want them to double-order unintentionally.

For example, remind the guest who orders the burger that fries are already served with it and instead, recommend something else that will enhance the choices they have made like the Cajun-fried onion rings.

Consistency is key

It's important to know what the food and drinks should look like. If a salad is missing an ingredient or a dish has something served on the side, it should be obvious to all of your team – front and back of house. Consistency is key.

All present and correct

Ensure your guests have everything they need for when food arrives, such as correct cutlery, plate ware and condiments. Bring all the meals at the same time for every course and make sure those additional sides you recommended have not been forgotten and waiting in the kitchen.

Know your onions

Whenever possible, be in the know about when food and drinks are arriving at the table and be aware of who has ordered what. An amateur asks, "Who's having the pizza?" A professional knows who ordered what and knows when something is missing.

One less problem

When someone raises an issue, query or complaint, always respond in a positive and well-mannered way to help diffuse the situation.

Dismissing a request or an issue with the words "no problem" is a problem because it has a tone of insincerity or sarcasm. Instead, say "My pleasure", "I completely understand" or "You're very welcome" as a more genuine and reassuring message.

Mind your manners

The golden rule of table etiquette is to always wait until everyone has finished his or her meal.
I know, it seems too basic to even list, but as a slow eater I can confirm far too often entire tables of plates are cleared around me. Don't make anyone feel uncomfortable, that they have eaten too fast, or that they are eating too slowly!

Ask the awkward question

Sometimes a guest has finished their meal but left plenty of food still on the plate. When clearing a plate with lots left on it, always enquire how their meal was. It can feel uncomfortable asking this question, but you need an opportunity to rectify something if it wasn't right.

STEP 4 - THE PAYMENT

This is the sticking point that often takes a five-star experience down to a three-star one – guests simply wanting to pay the bill.

Now, if you've found out what your guests' plans are, you should be aware if they are under any time constraints. Beyond that, if you have produced the bill, ensuring all is present and correct, be sure to be on standby ready to take a swift payment.

A Negative Experience

The waiter clears our plates and then without any requests from our party, slams the bill down in front of the person celebrating their birthday. The staff member then proceeds to forget all about us as we sit there waiting for the payment to be taken. We still feel like an inconvenience and now feel embarrassed that the birthday girl has been given the bill. We were going to get desserts but are now being pushed out the door. Disaster meal from start to finish! We feel frustrated, embarrassed, disappointed and bewildered!

A Positive Experience

The team member brings over the bill and places it on the table by the family member who requested it. The team member apologises again for the mix up with the garlic bread and has removed it from the bill.

Once he has seen we are ready for payment, he promptly brings over the card machine and processes the payment. The whole experience has been sublime. Even when the mistake happened it was rectified quickly, and the waiter seemed in control at all times. We haven't waited for anything and feel so well taken care of. The service charge doesn't begin to cover the efforts we have received so we decide to leave a tip on top. We feel utterly delighted, happy, relieved, and content!

SALES PRO TIPS

The good, the bad, the ugly

We often attract opinions, complaints and "helpful" suggestions on the restaurant floor, some good, some bad and yes, some ugly. Always listen, take these seriously (*not personally*) and address them professionally. Hearing feedback, even when we don't like what we hear, should never be dismissed. It may sound trivial to you but it certainly isn't trivial to your guests.

Standby for action

Once a dining experience appears to be coming to an end (for example, the desserts and coffees are finished and no one wants to order anything else), stand by and keep an eye on your guests.

Don't hover long enough to make people feel they are being watched or hurried but have a clear view of your table so they are not left feeling forgotten about. Be prepared for the universal "check, please" sign!

Check, please!

If a few people signal for the bill, print it, double-check it's correct and find a neutral place on the table to leave it. A handwritten "thank you" on the bill has been shown to raise tips and give a personalised approach to a formal process. Try not to stand over and put pressure on guests to pay, especially when they are figuring out the tip or trying to split the bill.

Just split it

When large groups of friends dine out together, one of the most annoying parts of the meal is when it comes to splitting the bill and paying individually. By having simple procedures in place, you can make it easy to split the bill and take multiple payments. Remember, this is near the end of the guest journey, therefore, there is little time left to turn a negative experience back into a positive one. Be there to help solve any problems that occur.

Prince Charming!

Exceptional service is about an incredible experience from start to finish, it's not about turning on the charm and becoming Prince (or Princess) Charming when it's tip time.

No one is fooled by a last-minute quip or smile; you want your guests to feel welcome and attended to at all time. Always bring the change back to the table – never assume it will become a tip!

STEP 5: THE DEPARTURE

This is the last step to the guest experience – we must not let ourselves down now! We want to leave our guests feeling appreciated, happy and welcomed for their next visit. That feeling is what will remain with them when they talk about your business to their friends and family, when they write their reviews and when they consider heading out to dine again.

A Negative Experience

Once we have paid, every member of staff instantly ignores us. We cannot wait to leave this place and to jump online and write a review so we can warn others about what a terrible waste of time this place is. As we get up to leave, no one says thank you, no one says goodbye. We leave feeling disappointed, sad, frustrated and angry.

A Positive Experience

As we get up to leave, we receive a fond farewell from both our waiter and another team member. They tell us about a Brazilian BBQ and Cocktail night that is happening next month and give us an invitation.

We feel like this place has really enjoyed looking after us and we feel special to be invited back! What a lovely gesture and a fond farewell from everyone. We can't wait to leave a glowing review and return again soon. We feel relief, joy and satisfaction!

SALES PRO TIPS

Thank you!

If you do receive a tip – a great one, a good one, or even a bad one – try not to overreact and make anyone feel embarrassed or uncomfortable. Simply say, "Thank you very much. I hope we will be welcoming you back again very soon."

Be back soon

If you can, have something to tell your guests about. Perhaps a special cuisine night is in the calendar in the coming months, or for Independence Day you'll be hosting a big party. For this, use The Service Laps:

Look – what event do you think would interest them?
Ask – if they have heard about your special event or if they enjoy a particular cuisine.
Propose – tell your guests the main details of the event.
Serve – tell them how they can find out more or make a reservation.

Goodnight

Every guest that leaves should do so with a fond farewell, so it's everyone's job to keep an eye on tables preparing to leave. If they are standing, putting on coats, perhaps saying goodbye to one another, be sure to say farewell to them too.
It's the last touch-point of their experience with you so be sure it is positive, friendly and leaves a lasting memory. Remember, we are in the business of *repeat business!*

OVERVIEW: THE GUEST JOURNEY

Take a handful of interactions from the positive journey examples and some from the negative ones.
This is life in the *real* world. Unfortunately, it can take just one negative interaction to ruin and cancel out a multitude of positive ones. Heart breaking, but true!

Our guests can endure a rollercoaster of highs and lows during their time with us. Their emotions and feelings bounce between good and bad, but the bad ones tend to linger for a while. No one will be rushing back to your restaurant after they were sat waiting to order a drink for an hour, it doesn't matter how smiley the door host was!

By understanding your guest journey and ensuring time and time again it is positive for the guest at every stage, it builds trust and rapport between your business and the guest. The guest begins to feel they know, like and trust you and this paves the way for successful sales through exceptional service.

Of course, your team members already serve your guests, answer their questions, take their orders, and deliver their food and drinks to them.

But by adding the *right* questions followed by the perfect proposal, it will change the dynamic completely. In fact, there are three opportunities where you have the chance to create exceptional service and make good sales by using the Service LAPS:

- **When you approach the guests to take their order**

- **When the first round of drinks needs replenishing**

- **When they have finished eating their main courses**

At each of these points, you have the opportunity to follow the Service LAPS process by guiding your guests, giving them fantastic options and using menus as props, recognising opportunities, and offering extras to enhance their experience.

Remember, relaxed, happy and content guests will be more open about sharing what they like when asked and will, in turn, be more receptive about what proposals your team can provide for them.

MANAGEMENT VS LEADERSHIP

As juniors and trainees, our job was to become good at our jobs – and that's just what we did. As a waitress, I was taught how to clear tables faster, more quietly and more efficiently. I was taught to carry plates and walk really fast without even a garden pea rolling off. I learnt ingredients and recipes and allergy details to ensure when I was asked a question I knew the answers.

As a bartender, I had to study mixology and learn hundreds of recipes, measurements, garnishes and ingredients off by heart. I had to know how to pour with speed and precision, add up bar bills in my head and multi-serve guests dotted all around the busy island bar, sometimes stacked four deep.

It was mastering how to do my job and do it better than anyone else that led me into a management role – and that's where my learning almost ground to a halt. Suddenly, I was in charge of the people who did the job I used to do but no one was there to show me *how* to manage them.

Time and time again we promote the best bartender or the best waitress the business has, rewarding them with more responsibility and more pressure to perform, but with little know-how and even less guidance on how to do it successfully. That's exactly how we end up as managers and not leaders.

We as business leaders must understand that high performance and high profits can only happen if we take charge and implement change. We need to develop our skills so we show those around us how to do something and have the knowledge to develop skills in others.

We are so busy managing to get everything done, we overlook our need to lead those around us. And because we were able to do their job better than anyone, we end up doing their job for them through frustration. We micromanage our team, making the drinks because it will be faster, dealing with the complaints because it will be easier and taking the orders because we know the menu better.

What we need to do is go through a transition – some people do this with ease, whereas for others, it's far more of a struggle. We are now no longer responsible for doing the job but rather responsible for the team who are there to do the job.

What we see time and time again in our industry are the best people being taken out of their role, given more money, more responsibility and told to manage without being taught how to *lead*. Leadership, like sales, is a skill like any other.

We need to learn to lead, practice how to lead and develop our own leadership style. But if we are only ever told to "manage", that is all we'll ever be able to do.

THE POWER OF THE PRE-SERVICE MEETING

"Tell me and I will forget. Show me and I will remember. Involve me and I will understand"

Taking time to empower your team on a daily basis can be the difference between winning at Sales Through Service and slipping back into the old ways. Ensuring your team is set for success via a pre-service meeting not only gives them clarity in their mission but also will instill confidence to do it well.

The pre-service meeting happens ten minutes before the doors open and brings everyone together to get them on board with what the service will look like. It takes a Manager to step into the role of Leader to make this happen though. So what are the key elements to making your pre-service meetings a success?

Motivate

"Hi everyone, hope you're all doing ok..." Wow – watch out Tony Robbins, there's a new Mr Motivator in town. This is the time to energise and motivate your team, before they go out and try to achieve everything you're asking of them. Get yourself in the "go get 'em" game. Smile, speak with passion, speak from the heart, and truly believe with full positivity that tonight, even with umpteen challenges, will be another opportunity to excel.

Set your team up for success with motivation at the beginning of each and every service. You want your team feeling pumped and energised – ready to welcome in each and every guest and tackle the challenges that will be heading their way.

We all are incredibly busy and there is always something that will be tugging at our time. But stay committed to your pre-service meeting every, single, day. Believing that there "isn't enough time" will rob your team of training, your guests of exceptional service and your business' bank balance of thousands. *Make the time.*

Educate

No one is an expert in your products without a little effort. The reason so many people struggle to sell is because they don't believe in or understand what they are selling. Don't overwhelm your team but do select a great dish to be recommended and a great beverage too. What is unique about it? Who is it perfect for? What are some interesting points of knowledge about it?

Be sure everyone is aware of the products you really want your guests to enjoy today and *why*. Are you aiming to wow our guests with a multitude of courses and extras?

Perhaps you're providing them with a fast-paced delicious feast, as so many will be off to see a show at the theatre next door. What do your guests want and how can you best serve those needs?

Empower

Empower your team to learn from their own mistakes and serve them up a Success Sandwich. Ok, I'll admit this is sometimes called a S*** (rude word) sandwich, but I much prefer a Success Sandwich.

This is where you give a brief overview of what happened on the last service (or if it's a particularly different service day like a Saturday, you might cover what went down a week ago). You start by highlighting some of the positives of the service, what went right and why.

Followed by the challenges that the team faced, what went wrong and why. By learning from your mistakes you avoid your restaurant losing money and goodwill that it doesn't need to. Finally, cover some more success and how to overcome challenges if they show up again. Focus on the amazing possibilities this service has to offer and get everyone in a positive headspace.

Track

Who went above and beyond last time? Celebrate (and reward) their success. Plus, set the stall out for what you need from your team during this service.

What rewards are up for grabs for success tonight? Tell your team what you'll be tracking and what they need to do to create success.

Next, get the team talking about how you'll create success as a team. Bartenders, what is the speciality cocktail tonight? Are you ready with all the ingredients, glassware and garnishes? Front of house, do you know what it tastes like? What it looks like? What ingredients are in it? How it is served and what groups of guests will really enjoy it?

Chefs, what speciality dishes (that are high in GP) are in stock and great to serve for guests in a rush? Front of house team, do you know what great side dishes can be recommended to go with this dish? Bartenders, what premium wine is the perfect accompaniment?

What does each department need from the others? Chefs need the food to be taken away quickly and efficiently. They need the orders to be complete and correct. They need dirty plates cleared and brought back again.

Bartenders – what do they need? Maybe they want to recommend Grey Goose vodka tonight as you're holding too much stock of that at the moment. They need wine glasses polished and extra garnishes cut – can the KPs help with that?

Front of house – what do they need?

They need to know when the kitchen is starting to get slammed, when there may be inevitable delays on the food. By being aware, they can pre-empt any frustrations from the guest and pre-warn them that their food may take a few minutes longer.

When you bring everyone together and communicate to them as a team, get them talking as a team and understanding one another, the service runs smoother, your team will be happier, and the guests are taken better care of.

Confessions of a Sales Pro

"I had my first job in a restaurant aged 17 as a table busboy at a high-end Italian in Kingston. I helped out most weekends and in my summer holidays. The tips were huge and the team were experienced, all I had to do was scrape and stack the plates in the kitchen, run the desserts and try not to break or drop anything! Pretty soon after my 18th birthday, I was unexpectedly "promoted" to being a waiter (because someone didn't show up for their shift) and I remember I didn't really have a clue what I was doing. Growing up my family had never taken me to places like this, I would never have been able to afford to eat in a place like this – so the rules of the dining room were like an alien language to me! I would clear plates before others were finished, I would try and carry a million things at once, I panicked at the thought of opening a champagne bottle, and I would shy away from answering any question with an "everything's great" reply because I couldn't really pronounce the specials – let alone know what went in them.

Now fast forward twenty years I am a General Manager and I understand some of the young people I employ are just like I was – completely unaware of the right way to do things because they have never been accustomed to "this way". It's not their fault, but it is my job to ensure they not only understand the rules, they understand why they are so important."

SALES PRO TIPS

Know your numbers

Working out what products and dishes are most profitable is essential when it comes to sales success. If you don't feel confident about understanding your GP (gross profit) or your cost of sales – don't worry, you're not alone! We have created a simple to follow cheat sheet and calculator for you to download for free: **www.thehospitalitymasters.com**

The three elements

Throughout the guest journey, we cannot afford to only sell by chance. Selling requires effort, knowledge and energy, but should always be friendly rather than forced.

A waiter who is professional and knowledgeable, but without any friendliness comes across as rude.

A waitress who is professional and friendly without any knowledge is unhelpful.

A bartender who is friendly and knowledgeable but without any professionalism is probably unemployed!

As sales and service people, we must remember the three elements of our roles: We need **knowledge**, **professionalism** and **friendliness** in equal measure in order to be exceptional.

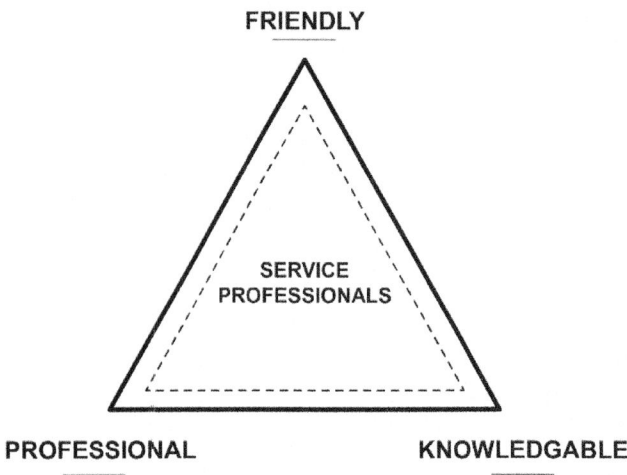

THE SERVICE TRIANGLE

Incentivise your team

You need to educate and motivate your team into *wanting* to improve their service and sales.

Unsurprisingly, we have found most team members are motivated by financial incentives. Of course, there are other techniques – gamification and prizes – but money always works well.

The information we laid out at the start of the book shows how an increase of £5 per head will benefit your business, but it's also easy to show your staff how it will benefit them through increased tips and service charge.

Measure and track results

What gets measured gets done, so you need to monitor all your server's sales. An easy way is through the spend per head but like all sales territories, some sections in the restaurant may offer better opportunities to sell than others, so you may need to make allowances for this.

THE SERVICE LAPS

To make excellent sales, your servers need to follow a system each time they approach a table – The Service LAPS. This four-step system is a constant loop of your section and your guests. Not every loop or lap will require an action, but we should be regularly be looking and ready to follow on with the next steps. Let's explore the four steps a little further.

STEP 1: LOOK

Observe your tables and understand what is happening with your guests. These are things you probably do anyway as part of your everyday service; we want you to really take notice and then act upon what you have seen.

STEP 2: ASK

Following on from your observations, a relevant question is needed. This is your opportunity to find out what your guests may need or like, which is essential for selling – we don't want to push something they're not interested in. For example, wine menus being offered to beer drinkers, fish dishes being proposed to steak lovers. We want to find out what the guests would like and be able to plant a seed of what they may like to order. It's all in asking the right questions.

STEP 3: PROPOSAL

Following on from asking the right questions is the proposal. This is where you propose or suggest something to your guests that you believe they will really enjoy. The proposal involves a recommendation and, if required, a description of the product – empower the guest to know more. Remember, if they don't know about a product, they certainly won't buy it. Missing the opportunity to propose guarantees failure 100% of the time.

STEP 4: SERVICE

This occurs naturally when your team follow your mapped-out guest journey. The guest still places the order (something they were going to do anyway) but you have now guided them to order the perfect products for them.

By following the four steps of The Service LAPS, you'll make excellent sales through service. When using this process, team members will increase their tips, the spend per head will improve and, ultimately, the business will experience a rise in turnover.

Rather than overwhelming your team with opportunities, begin with making the most out of the obvious ones. Remember, regular small changes can harvest great results.

Let's now take a deeper look into the four steps of The Service LAPS.

STEP 1: LOOK

"Look, and look again. What do your guests need, how can you serve?"

Team members need to look at what is happening on their tables and then know how to proactively respond. What we are trying to achieve is a more personalised and individual service for the table. It's not about selling what we want to sell them but finding out what products they want to buy and what products they need to try.

Learning to look and read your guests

By reading your guests successfully, you can guide and advise them throughout their time in the restaurant. It's a tricky skill to learn but if you look for clues in your guests, they are often there to be found. It may be in the clothes they are wearing, the energy and volume of the table or the props they have brought with them (the business meeting with laptops and paperwork vs the hen party with novelty t-shirts and banners!).

Ultimately, you want to offer the guests a personalised service by adapting your style and recommendations to suit each table. People visit restaurants for different reasons and as such will expect different styles of service. Your ability to read a table will help determine how successful you are at satisfying your guests.

In reality, reading a table takes seconds. Are they friends or strangers? Are they there for fun or business? Is this meal something social with the group doing a lot of drinking or is it a quick lunch or non-alcoholic dinner? Are they attending a funeral or heading to a Blues Brothers costume party?

These are things you *need to know* as a server because they affect everything from the time guests spend at the table to the bill and the kind of products they order.

If a guest grabs a wine list or starts ordering drinks straight away, focus your efforts in that area initially and be ready to take the next steps in the LAPS process. Are they heading to the theatre or a concert?

If guests are very dressed up and dining early, they may have another event to get to, and may require a speedier service from you. Understanding cooking times and therefore coordinating the length of their stay will be crucial. If they are business people who look like they are on a lunch break, again, speedier service is what they need.

Reading (and understanding) multiple groups – who all have different expectations – at the same time while making each of those groups feel like they are your number one concern can be a challenge. Be aware you are managing "the gap" between your guests' expectations and what you can actually deliver.

The wider the gap the more likely there are to be problems and having a "guest at risk". The guest can end up "at risk" of being disappointed, having a bad experience, and even making a complaint or writing a bad review (we'll cover how to deal with a guest at risk later).

Look at what is needed on the table

At this first stage of the Service LAPS, you need to simply look at the table and decide what is needed. This will present opportunities to sell and to serve. The obvious things to look for are:

Are they waiting to be seated?
Are they ready to order?
Do their drinks need topping up?
What stage of the meal are they at?
Are they finished eating?
Are they ready to order desserts and coffee?
Do they need the bill or are they waiting to pay?

These situations will create an opportunity to be attentive to your guests and to find out what they want or need. By looking at your tables and noting body language, eye contact and general remarks, you can make service feel natural and not mechanical. And by building positive rapport at the table, it will be easier to make great recommendations.

During the service, it's important to keep an eye on your guests and be mindful of their body language. Happy guests do a good job of showing they are happy; some indications include:
Relaxed bodies and shoulders
Leaning back
Smiling and laughing, having high-energy conversations
Openly engaging with others on their table and staff

Likewise, dissatisfied guests do a good job of showing how they feel:

Are they looking around?
Are they leaning forward looking annoyed?
Do they look bored or sullen?
Are their eyes darting around the restaurant?
Are they constantly looking toward the kitchen?
Are they shifting around a lot in their seats?
Have they left food on their plates?

This isn't a game of poker... people tend to be fairly obvious in their body language. Because people often resist speaking up when they're unhappy with their meal, you need to learn to detect when guests are unhappy. Even if it's not your assigned table, you should alert someone or deal with it yourself.

Your body language

Remember that "look" is a two-way street – the guests will be looking at the team members too.

Everyone who works in front of house positions is visible and your body language is important to be aware of. It all starts with a genuine smile, an energetic walk and an open body showing you're being attentive at all times. Is your body language saying you are open and warm or it accidentally saying you are closed and cold?

Ultimately, you want to build trust and rapport with your guests. Your body language changes your tone of voice and your mindset. Your guests will feel connected to what you're offering them, they will have a good emotional response and, in turn, feel more appreciated and cared for.

You also want to nod your head and smile, so they nod their heads and smile back at you and accept what you are saying. You need to listen to them and be open and, in return, they will listen and be open with you. When we create personalised and efficient conversations, we open up opportunities for exceptional service and sales to take place.

Identifying the host – decoding the dynamics of the table

There's usually someone in charge of the table. Generally speaking, it's the person who organised the reservation and the person who is paying the bill. Identifying this person is important as they set the tone for what happens on the table.

The clues to identifying this person are numerous; from the name that the table is booked under or the first one to speak. They may ask about specials or are more proactive in the initial interaction with your team members.

Whatever the host does, the guests follow suit. Not only does the host of the table decide if everyone is having wine but they also decide how many courses the table has, including deserts and coffee.

If the host orders an appetizer, then the rest of the guests generally will too. If you can look and establish who that person is, it will be easier to make sales as you can direct your questions and proposals at them directly. This is especially true with large parties of four or more, where everyone usually looks for one person to take the lead.

STEP 2: ASK

Never be afraid to ask. The risk of guests saying *"no"* is worth the opportunity of guests saying *"yes"*

The second stage in our LAPS process is the Ask. Remember, if you don't ask, you won't sell.

By asking questions and being concerned with finding out more from your guests, your guests feel taken care of, the business you work for thrives and the front of house team earn more in tips, commission or service charge. You can do this by using your insider knowledge, expertise and understanding what your guests want and matching that up to what is on offer.

But how do you know what your guests want and like? You ask! Asking the right questions at the right time can build rapport, increase trustworthiness and reduce resistance.

Now, no one wants to feel forced to make purchases they don't want or need. So in order to establish what they like or want, you have to ask them. We don't mean this in the form of interrogation though, it's the art of *gentle* questioning and asking the *right* questions.

This is an added step and the small change to what you may usually do at the table. It takes a few extra seconds but it will transform the way you interact with the guests and make your life much easier and your service more successful.

You want to achieve two things with your question:
Establish what the guests like so you can easily carry out step three of the LAPS and propose something suitable.

Plant seeds in the guests' head of what they might like to order by making them think about it.

Remember, it's a balancing act between effective sales through service which is subtle and helps guide the guests to decisions and going all out on recommendations and turning them off. We do this successfully by asking a relevant golden question.

Relevant golden questions are a powerful and effective sales technique – you are warming the guest up to get the right answer. Your question has the guest thinking "yes" and by thinking about it, they begin to *crave it*.

A good example of this would be asking "who likes chocolate with their coffee?" Instantly the guest is starting to think about delicious chocolate alongside a fabulous coffee. Yes and yes!

Chances are everybody on the table likes chocolate, so you have established they like chocolate and you have got them thinking about chocolate.

Then you will follow up with a proposal of something delicious and chocolatey from your menu. They are far more likely to say "yes" than if you came and presented them with the menu before walking away.

There are a whole variety of different situations that you will see in your restaurant every day where you can find ways to ask the right question. If you can use positive body language by smiling and nodding when asking it will further increase your chances of getting a positive outcome.

Remember what was mentioned earlier in the book – we are very fortunate. In our industry, we have guests walking through the door who definitely want to buy something.

It's simply our job as the front of house team to recommend a great option for them and make great suggestions throughout their time in the restaurant. If we don't tell them about it, they won't know about it. And if they don't know about it, they're certainly not going to order it. Sell outside the box.

Here are some examples of how most servers will approach a table after the main course has been cleared:
Would you like to see a dessert menu?
Would you like a coffee?
Can I get you another drink?

The problem is, there are only two answers to these questions – "yes" or "no". Once you have asked a yes or no question, the guest is going to go through a series of pros and cons in determining the answer to the question. This makes it much easier for the guest to say "no".

You can avoid this situation by asking a golden question. Golden questions trigger more positive associations which lead to more positive responses:

"Who likes desserts?"
"Who enjoys coffee with their desserts?"
"How did you enjoy your cocktail? Same again or would you like to try something new?"

Unless a guest is particularly stubborn, it's hard to give a one-word or negative answer to these questions!

Now you need to think about all the different ways you can do this throughout the course of the service. If you can ask a guest a relevant golden question you are more likely to get the guest thinking "yes". And if you can get the guest thinking "yes", they are more likely to want to order one of your proposals.

Let's look at some examples...

Dessert sales

You approach the table with the dessert menus in your hand. Most order takers will say, "Would you like to see the dessert menu?" This is a closed question and the guest can easily say "no". This is not necessarily bad service but it's not going to help your sales (or service tips!). You need to ask a *relevant golden* question. For example, when you bring the dessert menus to the table, ask the guests, "Who likes chocolate?"

What does that question do? Well, first off it establishes whether or not the guests like chocolate or not. As we know from experience, most people do like chocolate so it will most likely gain a positive response. But the more important thing that's happening is the associations in the guests' minds. The thought of eating chocolate will elicit a positive emotion and the guests will begin to crave chocolate.

Technically, the brain releases a feel-good chemical designed to make you feel good called dopamine.

You're getting the guests to think, "Yes, I like chocolate." Which is the answer you want to your golden question! This then opens the door to a follow-up proposal and the chances of making a dessert sale have dramatically increased.

Coffee sales

Coffee is another great product for open-ended questions. When you go up to a table with the dessert menu, before you even speak about desserts, ask this golden question: "Who would enjoy a frothy cappuccino with their dessert?"

Of course, everyone enjoys a cup of coffee with their dessert. Take your coffee order before you even start talking about desserts. Now you've landed a coffee order and because the guests are going to be sitting there for a while longer drinking their coffee, they're going to need a dessert.

Then you go ahead and plant that golden question, "Who likes chocolate?"

Throughout the duration of the meal, there are opportunities to ask the right golden questions that you need to be on the lookout for.

Confession of a Sales Pro

"Before learning Sales Through Service, I would always feel clumsy when trying to sell to my guests. Understanding and adding an "ask" made me feel more in control and helped me build better rapport – and quickly! Just by asking something as simple as "are you a fan of craft beers?" would spark great conversations. Beer drinkers tend to have an opinion on craft beers, whether they like them or not! If they say "yes" I spring into telling them about my top three craft choices this week. If they say "no" I tell them all about my premium lagers. I've had a 100% success rate from people trying something other than the standard pint on tap. I've learnt more about my guests and regularly sell out of our most premium products."

STEP 3: THE PROPOSAL

"If your guests don't know about it, they certainly won't buy it!"

The proposal is suggesting something to the guest that you believe they will like (you have already asked the right questions to give you the inside track). Proposing is about helping your guests make informed decisions towards better products while increasing sales. But we don't want the guests suffering bill shock and feeling ripped off, so always suggest appropriately priced Items. This is about exceptional guest experiences, not about shaming or pushing people into making choices they don't really want.

If you have asked your guests if they like steak and they do, don't be afraid to recommend a couple of steak options from your menu. Your proposal should be based on something you've asked and something they've answered. It's not about just springing the most expensive dish into the conversation and hoping for the best!

To propose these helpful recommendations effectively to your guests, you need to:

- **Choose your words carefully**
- **Have good product knowledge**
- **Have a professional and friendly approach**

Choose words that paint a picture

Simply saying something is "amazing", "incredible" or "everyone loves it" by itself is *meaningless*. These are ineffective adjectives and you could be describing anything. Be sure to really paint a picture for your guests.

Use words like tender, crisp, rich, sweet and smooth to help paint the picture in their mind. If you can get the guest to imagine eating and enjoying the item you are describing, you have made the sale.

Choose words that Inform

Each word you choose should give the guest more information about the meal.

Specific descriptive words will help guide the undecided into the decision. Perhaps the item is from a particular region, is in season at the moment or is the chef's speciality.

Use words that emphasise the strengths of the meal
Tell the guests what makes the item you are describing better than what they can get elsewhere. Let them know your steaks are aged, that your vegetables are fresh and steamed, that the coffee is freshly ground and from which part of the world.

Choose proposals based on the guests

Looking at the guests at your table will give you guidance on what items to sell and which words to choose.

A table of rugby players ordering jugs of beer are unlikely to be interested in a side salad but may be interested in sides of onion rings, chicken wings and extra garlic bread with their mains.

A group of business people discussing deals may prefer options that are light and fresh, rather than anything too full of carbohydrates that can bring on yawns and feeling sluggish. Keep on top of coffees, speciality teas and mineral waters – these are great ways to sell and serve what your guests *really* need.

A couple with young children may prefer to have their starters brought out with their kids' main meals and their mains alongside their kids' desserts. Once the kids are finished, perhaps offer some colouring to keep them busy and allow the adults some quality time together over a dessert or two. Giving your guests the options to enjoy their time with you the way they want to is a sure-fire way of building positive experiences, loyalty and repeat business.

Remember, the proposal is about enhancing your guests' experience. If they are in a rush for a show at the theatre, recommend something tasty and quick. The best dish in the world won't be enjoyed if it needs to be rushed. You may lose an upsell once but build a loyal guest for many years.

Your product knowledge is crucial

You can't effectively propose and sell products you don't know. So it's important that you learn about your menu and how to describe the main dishes you wish to sell. By knowing your products you will be more confident in your job role, provide better suggestions, and satisfy customer expectations better than ever before.

When specific words are used to describe items from your menu, the guest then begins to imagine how the dish will look or taste as your description begins to stimulate the pleasure centres in their brain.

Words that help you serve and sell

Take, for example, something like a hot chocolate. When described with adjectives like hot, rich, thick, gooey, chilled, layered, creamy, or frothy, it takes on an entirely new meaning.

You should always focus on what you are trying to sell and how you are selling it to the people you are selling it to. Trying to convince someone to buy something they have no interest in will waste your time and hurt your credibility.

Confessions of a Sales Pro

"I have always made recommendations to my customers, so I kind of thought I knew all about how to make better sales. What I have learned is that I wasn't tailoring my suggestions to my guests – I was always just telling them about what I like. Sometimes it would connect, be a suitable suggestion and lead to a sale. But most of the time it would result in a response like "Oh I don't like cheese" or "I can't handle spice" or "Vodka gives me headaches". Now I know to do a bit of fact-finding first and have plenty of useful suggestions up my sleeve (or in my apron). Everyone is different so I realise now it's not just about me and my favourites it's about asking the customer and finding out theirs!"

QUICK STEPS TO SUCCESS

Recommending a Main #1

Often your guests will ask you the question, "What's good here?"

This is a *golden* opportunity. You should be able to describe two or three popular items that you do really well or better yet, recommend something that you like.

Current approach: An order taker quickly replies to the guest, "Everything."

This is a terrible answer! It's unhelpful, lazy and doesn't assist the guest in making an informed decision.

Better approach: A sales professional replies with a relevant question, "Do you like Steak?" or "Do you like Seafood?" (or whatever your restaurant's speciality is).

And when you ask that question, the guests who like steak are thinking, "Oh yes! I like steak" and you're making them crave that steak or think about seafood.

Ultimate approach: The best approach is to ask, "Do you like Steak?" Followed up with a proposal if guests confirm they do like steaks, "How about one of our famous Argentinian steaks? They are incredibly tender and our sous chef grills them to perfection. They also go amazingly well with our delicious homemade fresh peppercorn sauce and a glass of our Spanish Rioja."

Recommending a Main #2

Addressing the people who said "yes" to Seafood

Current approach: "We have lots of great fish dishes on our menu."

Better approach: "Our fish is freshly caught and is our Chef's speciality."

Ultimate approach: "Our head chef is famous for her seafood, it's her speciality. She only uses freshly caught fish and her seafood gumbo is overflowing with shrimp, fish and delicious flavours. It's one of our bestselling dishes and often sells out before the end of service."

Drink sales

You've looked and noticed that your guest needed another glass of wine.

Current approach: "Can I bring you another glass of wine?" That is a close-ended question and there are only two answers, "Yes" or "No".

Better approach: "How did you enjoy that wine? Can I bring you another glass of the same or would you like to try something different this time?"

Ultimate approach: "How did you enjoy that wine? Can I bring you another glass of the same or would you like to try something different this time? I have a great Rioja, which will go well with the steak you have ordered. It's our featured wine this week."

This is a great example of the service LAPS at work. You've looked and noticed that the guest needed another glass of wine. You've asked them the right question to get them thinking "Yes" and made a qualified proposal. The guest is now likely to say "Yes!"

STEP 4: THE SERVICE

"Exceptional sales come from exceptional service"

The fourth step of the LAPS process is *service* (not sales!). That's because exceptional sales come as a *result* of excellent service. You need to create a culture of exceptional service within your business for your team to thrive in sales. In my first book "The Five Star Formula" I do a deep dive into building a positive culture.

The expectation of the level of service is laid out in your guest journey.

There's no getting away from how important *sales* are to your business but without our guests *enjoying* the service we provide them, we have no business at all!

The service we give our guests – or as some may call it, the *hospitality* – is the thread that runs throughout the experience and pulls it all together.

When we train front of house teams either through digital learning or in-person, we take them through the steps of the Service LAPS and get them to work through it within their restaurant's guest journey. Although the main steps are often similar to every team, every venue and every concept is unique and special in *what* they do and, of course, *how* they do it.

Once you get used to using the Service LAPS, we suggest you look at our website for many additional ideas on how to use them and additional opportunities for your team to learn and develop their skills. But for now, just get going with the basics.

So what *really* makes exceptional service? Service excellence is about delivering your guests' expectations and hopefully exceeding them! Every restaurant (or bar, hotel, pub, etc.) has its own unique brand, vibe and style, which the service should feel *appropriate* for. As the business leader, it's important to understand the brand promise your restaurant makes in regard to service and the related customer expectation.

You need to be crystal clear about your guests' expectations while also being true to the integrity of your restaurant's brand.

This includes creating a positive work environment for your team as well as meeting and exceeding your profit objectives. Getting your service fine-tuned to your guests' expectations takes effort and a desire to want to always improve.

Just like having your own unique guest journey, your service style will be unique as well. How you serve wine, how you serve food, how you serve cocktails – it all comes down to the right way for *you*. When we work one-to-one with businesses, we dive into the DNA of their business and create service standards and guides that are ideal for what you do to show you how to do it.

Whatever style of service you provide, there is an element of confidence required to be able to deliver really great service. You need to have the confidence to communicate well, ask the right questions and, of course, deal with rejection when it happens.

It's important to remember when you are serving your guests that you are their guide – give them options and, metaphorically speaking, give them the directions to follow. They may not always take you up on it but by being confident and professional in how you do it, they will still appreciate your efforts.

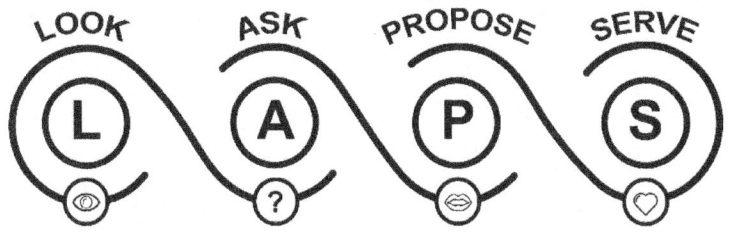

THE SERVICE LAPS

QUICK STEPS TO SUCCESS

Serve with purpose

Serving your guests with purpose is not about going through the motions and coasting through the service and watching the clock.

It means understanding not just what your guests need but what they *really want*. Having a purpose means being a useful addition to the experience, being their host and their guide throughout.

Serve with positivity

Being a positive person creates an atmosphere of happiness and optimism for everyone. It's not easy to always be positive, especially when the pressure is on, but if you can tackle everything with a positive outlook it makes challenges far easier to cope with.

Serve with passion

Serving with passion becomes infectious (in a good way!). It's wonderful if you have a passion for wine, or craft beers or even international cheeses. You can geek out to your heart's content and when your guests give you the green light, tell them all about your favourites.

Remember, most importantly is to have a passion for your guests and their wellbeing. Having a passion for people is the ultimate superpower when it comes to becoming a sales and service professional.

WHAT TO DO WHEN THINGS GO WRONG

"It's not about everything being perfect. It's about dealing with every situation and the challenges – perfectly."

Once you have created your guest journey, it's not enough to simply understand the steps and hope that everything in your service flows without an incorrectly made cocktail or a missing side dish. Being successful in hospitality is not about getting it right every time but about coping well when things go wrong.

GUEST AT RISK

Now, I'm the first to admit that *no one* is perfect and conducting a 100% perfect service is certainly a rarity. So it's important to have systems and processes in place to rectify things when they go wrong. Of course, you want everything to go well all the time but let's bake a little reality into the situation for a second, your guests should (hopefully) understand that you're human and mistakes can happen. However, we must always be professional and know how to rectify situations when things go wrong. The customer is King (and Queen) after all.

You need your team to be alert, confident and ready to act if they need to. We call it "identifying a guest at risk". A guest at risk is someone who is unhappy with an aspect of his or her experience and may or may not complain to you at the time.

Look for signs of guests being impatient, frustrated or stressed. They may be complaining loudly to one another, folding their arms or looking around the restaurant. Guests at risk are not only detrimental to the atmosphere within your restaurant but are also a risk of damaging the reputation of your business. You should have a procedure in place for how these guests at risk are handled.

Why is it important that guest complaints are dealt with effectively?

Poorly handled complaints are one of the main reasons for guests not returning to an establishment. For every one complaint you get, it's estimated up to ten other guests would have had the same experience and chose not to say anything (most likely voting with their feet and never returning but probably leaving you negative TripAdvisor reviews anyway).

We used to say that one dissatisfied guest could tell up to 15 people. These days, with the power of the Internet they can tell 1000s at the press of a button.

If you grasp the significance of this, you can see the potential income you have at risk if complaints are not properly handled. You can also see the need to get aggressive about identifying and solving any potential difficulties before your guests even become aware of them.

A guest complaining is an opportunity to rectify a problem that many people may be experiencing. You don't want to ignore the complaint or dismiss it immediately. The only thing this will do is make the guest feel like their opinion is not valued and their custom unimportant.

There are just two goals when handling a guest at risk: Calm and reassure the guest and give them confidence that the situation has been understood and is in the process of being resolved.

Transform them from a guest at risk into a guest who will return as a guest once more. Remember, we are in the business of *repeat* business!

If you can't get them back, you at least want to make sure they don't go out and do any damage to your reputation. When handling complaints, there is only a win-win for you and the guest or lose-lose. If you can resolve the problem successfully, the guest will leave happy and will hopefully come back again – you both will win. If the problem is not handled well, the guest will never come back and may cause your business' reputation damage and, of course, you both lose.

Dealing with a guest complaint is not something that should be feared and as a restaurant manager, you need to be prepared to deal with complaints and issues at any moment.

Know your colour codes

With The Hospitality Masters, one of the tools we use to train front of house teams is a simple coding system to communicate with one another quickly and efficiently without any guests in earshot understanding the situation.

Code Amber

Awareness: You can see and sense the guests getting agitated and want to prevent the situation from escalating further. Perhaps there is a delay with their food, they're unhappy with the table, etc.

Action: It's important to be looking out for Code Ambers constantly. Team members must be ready to react to rectify the situation. Keep the guest informed of what you are doing to prevent a problem from escalating.

Code Red

Awareness: Things have already gone wrong – the wrong dish has been cooked or in the wrong way, the drinks order was incorrect, a side dish was missing, they have been waiting an extremely long time for their food, etc. A complaint or poor review is imminent.

Action: This usually requires a planned intervention and response. The complaint must be listened to, understood and rectified in a swift and exceptional manner.

Code Blue

Awareness: The situation has been dealt with – they have gone from a code red to a code blue.

Action: This usually means monitoring the guest for the rest of their meal. They are in recovery, so we need to make sure every other step in their journey goes exceptionally well.

How to deal with complaints effectively: The 3 Rs Common causes of complaints include:

Orders coming out wrong or with items missing
Waiting a long time for a bill.

Taking a long time to have payment collected.

All are easily done during a busy shift and quite common during a quiet shift too. If a team member receives a complaint, we suggest having a simple, memorable system for dealing with it. The 3 Rs is an easy 3-step process to implement and remember: Remove, Replace, Recover.

Step 1: Remove

Remove the offending item or whatever is causing the problem.

Step 2: Replace

Replace with the appropriate item or solution.

Step 3: Recover

Recover the situation by turning it around with a gesture – a free offering or a refund on the item(s).

By having this system in place, you are embracing the fact that things can and do go wrong at any time. The golden opportunity when things go wrong is having the action points in place to put it right in a way that satisfies the team member, the business and, most importantly, the guest. Empowering your front of house staff to deal with problems gives them responsibility and relieves you of added duties.

Frequently practising how to deal with difficult situations is the best way to learn. Often, we role-play with front of house teams in Sales workshops. We build up their confidence to deal with challenges.

By becoming superstars at doing things right when things go wrong, service (and sales) see rapid growth. It's quite common for the team members to end up earning more tips and restaurants getting better reviews because of the positive way they deal with issues.

Some simple rules to follow:

1. Listen and empathise with your guest

Failing to listen to the guest will only lead to the situation escalating, as their frustration will grow in an instant. You must always look interested in what they are saying – turn the tables and become the guest who is complaining, how would you feel if the manager wasn't taking things seriously or even listening?

2. Keep calm

Never lose your cool when dealing with a complaint. This may be difficult at times because of other stresses connected to the restaurant, but your professionalism has to kick in and you must stay calm or this will only make the situation worse.

3. Always attempt to understand

It can be automatic for you to become defensive whenever you are faced with a guest complaint.
But going into defense mode won't resolve the problem and could make matters worse. Good guest service when dealing with a complaint involves making a clear attempt to understand their frustration and the issue that they have.

4. Use your initiative

Each complaint is unique to the individual and it will serve you well to use your initiative with each complaint. For example, if the complaint is connected to something that you can physically change, such as unhappiness with the table or even a member of staff, then get it changed as quickly as possible.

This will help to reduce the tension and the guest will feel that their complaint was not only listened to but that the correct action was taken and they will still, in most instances, feel that the guest service was more than adequate.

Dealing with extremely difficult, rude or aggressive guests

The guidelines that we set out above can be implemented in most situations, but there may be times where a guest is simply obnoxious and extremely difficult to deal with. But there are still ways you can deal with them in a professional manner, no matter how bad the situation may appear to be. We do admit that this is something that can be quite difficult, but that's where your training in leadership really does come to fruition.

In this situation, it's best to deal with their issue as quickly as possible to prevent things from escalating any further. Leaving them to stew over their complaint will only lead to the tension inside them building even more and this will make your job of calming them and resolving the situation almost impossible.

If you find yourself in this situation, consider the following points:

1. Always keep control of yourself

This can be extremely difficult to do, especially if you are faced with a guest that is on a real tirade against you.

However, losing control of your temper will only make matters worse, so you *must* keep control of yourself at all times. Breathe and always think about what you are going to say before you go ahead and do so.

We are all guilty of speaking before we think, but that is not a sign of a good leader. Keeping control of your emotions paints you in a better light and it's harder for the guest to stay angry at you if you're not reacting in the way they expected.

If a guest is shouting, allow them to vent and let off that steam. In most cases, the initial bluster will blow over and they will then settle down and be easier to deal with. Not reacting and allowing them to finish will usually reduce the tension in the air.

2. Never take it personally

To help you to deal with these guests, never take what they say personally. They are venting at you because you represent the restaurant and they need to let off steam in some way. They are unhappy with the service or something connected to their experience at the restaurant, not you as a person.

3. Give a summary of the complaint

To show the angry guest you have listened, provide a summary of your understanding of the complaint after they have finished expressing themselves. It's important for your guest to see that you were paying attention and are taking their complaint seriously.

Rather than leaving yourself open to agreeing with what they said: "I understand the chicken was undercooked." You want to express that it was just their belief: "I understand *you feel* that your chicken was undercooked". You don't want to admit or agree to something without being confident of the facts!

4. Show sympathy and respect

Even though you may feel they don't deserve it, you must show the guest sympathy and respect for their complaint. Doing this creates a feeling that you are taking things seriously.

You don't have to provide them with a full, in-depth apology, but a simple statement that accepts they've had an issue and that you are sorry that this is the case will suffice. It's amazing how showing respect towards the guest can help to smooth things over enough for you to then be able to work with them towards a suitable resolution.

5. Work on the resolution

Turn the tables on the guest by asking them what they feel would be an adequate resolution.

You should also put forward your own ideas and then come to a satisfactory conclusion that improves the relationship with the guest rather than the restaurant.

6. Take a breather

Once you've finished dealing with the guest, take a few minutes to review how you handled the situation.
This will give you a chance to calm down, especially if you have been holding back some anger and frustration. You must allow those feelings to dissolve or else you will then take that attitude and anger back out into the restaurant, which is never good!

It will also give you the chance to decide if you did the correct thing and whether something needs to be changed immediately to prevent others from complaining about the same thing.

Averting Complaints

It's best to be aware of what could go wrong before it happens. You can do this by learning to read your guests and understand what their requirements may be. For example:

A group of older patrons who are dressed in formal attire may expect a more deferential and elegant style of service.

Cinema or theatregoers may expect (and require) a speedier type of service.

A table with young children may prefer children's meals to be served first to help keep them from getting bored or disruptive.

A couple on a date night (especially a first date) might want to be left alone to talk and connect with one another.

Someone working on a laptop may want service with a minimum of fuss and interruptions. (They probably won't be interested in appetizers that are best for sharing or learning a lot about the cocktail menu).
A younger group informally dressed might want a more informal and fun style of service.

You also need to be mindful of the time of day, the day of the week and even the weather outside to keep your service and recommendations relevant. Strong cocktails may be a better recommendation on a Friday night rather than a Sunday night!

THE POSITIVE SIDE OF COMPLAINTS

1. Guests that expect a lot from you force you to be your best

It's easy to get complacent and let standards and staff behaviour slip. Guests that demand a lot help keep you and your team focused. If you are honest with yourself it may identify weaknesses in your operation.

2. Every complaint is an insight into how to make your business better

People go out to have a good time. Since you are in the business of making guests happy, the comments and feedback you get are invaluable research on how to do your job and make your company better.

Demanding guests can drive you crazy sometimes but pleasing them is the only reason your restaurant exists and they are in the best position to tell you how you are doing at it!

Your guests will always see things that you will never notice. Rather than ignoring guests, embrace them and learn from the experience.

3. Guests are more likely to complain if they think you care and you'll listen

If you don't want to hear it, nobody will bother to tell you. The more interested you are in the truth of your guests' experience and the more receptive you are to suggestions on how you can do better, the greater the chances you will get feedback. Some will be good news, some will be bad news, but it's all news that will help you prosper. Ignore it at your peril.

4. Resolving complaints satisfactorily increases guest loyalty

Statistics suggest that if someone has a complaint that is handled well, they are more loyal than if they never had a complaint at all.

We're not suggesting that you make mistakes just so you can fix them – there are plenty of errors that will happen without any special effort!

Perhaps it's because handling a complaint well is a personal statement of caring that establishes more of a personal connection between the guest and the restaurant, but complaining guests can often become your most loyal patrons.

5. Some complaining guests care about you and your business

They want to make you aware so you know what's going on and give you the opportunity to fix it. To improve your business, there should be a record made of each complaint and what the resolution was – these could then be used in strategy and training sessions.

THE SMARTER WAY TO SERVE (AND SELL)

I have always been somewhat bewildered when I'm sat down in a restaurant and the smiley waiter brings over a huge jug of water and a huge basket of bread. I personally love fresh bread smothered in butter with a sprinkling of pepper and a dash of oil. Delicious! I can build up quite a thirst too whilst I am devouring the bread basket, so I chug on the tap water. I can tell you one thing that's happening – I'm not feeling hungry or thirsty anymore, and I haven't spent a penny!

The concerning thing is as I am enjoying the atmosphere, the music, and the ambience, the money I'm going to be spending in this restaurant is only going down. Full of bread and water, suddenly starters seem a little unnecessary – so straight to mains we go.

Any room for desserts? After all that bread? No, we'll skip it thanks. When we leave, what do we remember? The bread, the main, and how nice it was that they kept us topped up with free water. In a hurry to come back? Hmmm…maybe not.

As a restaurant, we must be focused on incredible service. But if we want our business to be here next year, rest assured, we need to be creating some incredible sales as well!

Water, water, everywhere!

Let's just turn off the water tap for a second and take a view at the Sales Through Service way. I know, I know, some people actually want tap water. But some people also don't mind singing at top of their lungs to a tiny faint dot, miles away, hoping that it *really is* Beyoncé. Yep, terrible seats at the back of stadiums do get purchased too, but I'm not concerned with them.

What about the guests that want the best? Those who want the mineral water – that enjoy the better, healthier taste of fresh spring water? When you greet your table, do so with the Ask: "May I bring still or sparkling mineral water to the table today?" Give them the option to choose and give them the opportunity to buy. Remember, your guests are here for an *experience* – it's your job to provide them with the best possible one.

Who's for wine?

Wine knowledge must be a priority for our bar teams and front of house staff. Even our chefs must be included – how else can we develop our food menus to complement our wine menus? Make it a team mission to sell more wine but more importantly, to sell better wine. Remember, we are unlocking the doors of our house tour and showing our guests to the best seats at the Beyoncé concert!

When it comes to wine, it's easy to feel intimidated or overwhelmed. No one, and we mean no one, is born a wine expert.

We all must put time and energy into improving our knowledge and developing a passion for our wines. This means talking about our wine offering every day during our pre-service meetings or occasionally organising a wine tasting delivered by a supplier. Being aware of exactly why each wine is special and what dishes each can be paired with is crucial for effective wine sales.

Don't start with trying to learn 28 different wines in one training session – our brains weren't built to retain that much information. Instead, adopt one red, one white and one rosé which are a little more premium than your house range and start to build your team's knowledge about just *those* three wines.

Focus on the wines on your list that are 20-25% above your house option (or the same increase on the average bottle you currently sell). If a bottle of your house red is £19, focus on a premium option that is around the £24 price point. You don't want to create bill shock with your guests – you want them to adore the wine and come back to visit you again.

The problem with wine tastings is that they can descend into a pompous ceremony quite quickly if the wine buffs in the team (if you have any) are not reeled in. Keep it simple:

Be familiar with the colour, the pronunciation, grape variety, vintage, and the country it's from.
Know the general flavour and the key tasting notes.

Understand what dishes it goes well with (ideally, allow your team to try the dish with the wine so they really understand *what* they are proposing to your guests).

Know an interesting fact or story as these tend to be easy to remember and easy to tell your guests about. Has it won an award? Is it limited in production? Is there an anecdotal story about the vineyard?

This book is not a wine reference guide but broadly speaking, wine is can be split into five categories:

Sparkling
White
Rosé
Red
Dessert

These can then be elaborated further into nine broader categories:

Sparkling Wine
Light-Bodied White Wine
Full-Bodied White Wine
Aromatic (sweet) White Wine
Rosé
Light-Bodied Red Wine
Medium-Bodied Red Wine
Full-Bodied Red Wine
Dessert Wine

Visit our website for some helpful downloads to help educate your staff and cut through the wine noise. If you feel you and your team would like to take part in one of our Sales Through Service Wine Masterclasses, get in touch at **www.thehospitalitymasters.com**.

The more your team knows about your wine, the better your presentation of that wine which will make it easier for your guest to take you up on your suggestion. If your team members shy away from questions about wine, your guests will very quickly think that your restaurant is not passionate (or knowledgeable) about wine so it may be safer to just stick to the mineral water.

This is a sales and service disaster! Educate your team to sell with confidence every day – if they have confidence in your wines, so will your guests.

If you focus your team on selling away from your house range and into more premium products, you will see sales rocket to a higher price range. It also gives the guest the impression that this is the type of restaurant that knows its wines and it's the norm to order it here.

You will be able to serve wine with more confidence from the first approach of the table, meaning wine can be enjoyed earlier in the meal, and it gives you more opportunity to sell more bottles further along in the guest journey.

Make no mistake, many people *want* luxury. They want unique experiences and they want to *feel* special. By building your credibility with your guests, they will feel more comfortable trying more extravagant options and celebrating more with a speciality wine.

Most importantly though, when we take the time to ask our guests about their preferences and we are empowered to make great proposals from our wine list, their experience is enhanced and they feel incredibly well looked after.

How to Implement

Which of your premium wine ranges (20-25% above your house options or above your current average) is the perfect recommendation for the following:

Beef dish
Fish dish
Chicken dish
Salad
Warm Summer day
Cold Winter evening

Having these as a basic guide is a great place to start in building up your team's knowledge.

SALES PRO TIPS

Use the word "Featured"
Ensure you have a *featured* wine of the week or month. Using the word "featured" in any product will help sell more of that item.

Identify the host

Be aware of the hierarchy of the guests when it comes to wine sales. First and foremost, identify the host or the most senior person who will be responsible for choosing the wine. You can do this by asking a relevant question as simple as, "Who is in charge of ordering the wine tonight?" This also achieves the previous point we made about giving your guests the impression that ordering a bottle of wine in your restaurant is the norm.

Present the wine menu

Place an open wine menu into their hands so they can adopt the responsibility of wine selection right away. Do so with friendliness and confidence – they need to feel your presence as a professional guide when it comes to the wine. Build the guests' confidence in you by asking relevant questions.

Be knowledgeable

At this point, be prepared with some relevant suggestions for them. If it's a hot Summer's day, recommend a light, refreshing, zesty white. If it's a chilly winter's day, a dark and fruity Shiraz.

Are they celebrating? Perhaps a fantastic bottle of fizz for the table?

If you think your guests have more refined tastes and are less price-sensitive, don't be afraid to suggest something which is higher quality and therefore more expensive. They always have the option of saying no, but by giving them the information and advising them well, you can create a better product sale. Don't show people directly to the nosebleed seats – Beyoncé's biggest fans are willing to pay more to have a better experience. Your guests are no different!

Current approach: "Good evening everyone and welcome to Cherry Jam, my name is Jess and I'll be your server this evening. Would anyone like to start with something to drink?"

Better approach: "Good evening everyone and welcome to Cherry Jam, my name is Jess and I'll be looking after you this evening. Before we dive too far into the menus, who is in charge of making your wine decisions tonight? Who can I leave the wine list with?"

Ultimate approach: "Good evening everyone and welcome to Cherry Jam, my name is Jess and I will be looking after you. May I ask what brings you here this evening?" Await with interest for their answer – remember you are putting the guest at the centre of the conversation.

Then add: "Before we dive into the food menus, who is in charge of making your wine decisions tonight?"

After handing it to that person, "Thank you, now while looking at the list, the Cape Merlot is by far the most popular choice in this restaurant and one of my favourites. It is also our *featured* wine this month.

The quality of this wine really delivers and it's great value. It has a great medium-bodied taste to it and goes perfectly with our chef's speciality, the roast Lamb. Please take a look, if you need any other suggestions, I would be happy to come back and check on you in a few minutes."

Remember when adopting Sales Through Service, it's important to make a qualified suggestion based on who is sitting at the table. It's not about just pointing to something more expensive! This is not about judging our guests but instead making a good guess at what would be a great option for them.

Let's look at two examples:

A group of friends enjoying lunch

You could ask, "Who enjoys Prosecco to start off with? Or perhaps our delicious and zesty Sauvignon Blanc?" This will plant the seed.

Prosecco would be a great place to start your suggestion as this has the ability to be paired with anything on your menu – fish as well as meat.

A group of business people for dinner

A group of four businesspeople sit down at the table, and mention they've been a long meeting all day and are excited to eat. Maybe you think they will order rump or fillet steaks, so the Cabernet would be a good suggestion. Something with depth and rich in flavour to accompany steaks and other meat dishes.

For additional free resources including management and sales training please visit our website: **www.thehospitalitymasters.com**

Chef's specialities

This could be one of the easiest and fastest sales boost for your team to adopt. Guests are often excited and romanced with the uniqueness and limited availability of specials. Your specials should be updated regularly – a specials board that never changes is certainly not very special at all!

I always want to know what the Chef's Specialities are. They are usually more ambitious than what I would attempt at home, come with unusual ingredients and flavours and feel like a luxury or treat. They do often come with a more premium price tag but there's no surprise or concern there. I want to try something special, so I'm prepared to pay for it!

Your specials should complement the theme or style of your restaurant. Have knowledge of the provenance of the food, the way it is prepared and the way it is cooked. Is the dish fresh, locally sourced, hand-reared, grass-fed or homegrown? Understand the unique properties and be sure to propose them with confidence to your guests. Food tastes better when you understand the story behind it.

It's important to note that your Chef's specialities must be profitable. This sounds obvious but I can assure you from working with many restaurant owners it's not always the case. Your chefs must understand the true costs of their ingredients and the labour costs involved with the preparation. Also, they must understand the costs can vary from season to season. There must be great profits baked into these dishes or you're doing your business and your entire team a disservice.

Getting your just desserts!

Having show stopping desserts in your restaurant is the gift that keeps on giving. You don't need to have a huge variety of desserts on your menu, in fact, too much choice has been proven to put people off from selecting a dessert.

Your dessert menu should be delicious, able to be produced at peak times without too much stress on your team and be profitable:

If your deserts are not delicious, you'll disappoint your guests and potentially sabotage a return visit (even if your mains were incredible).

If your desserts are not easy to produce in high volumes or speed during busy times, your team will not *want* to sell them. No one wants to deliberately slow down the guests or be wrestling with sinking soufflés when they're under pressure.

If your desserts aren't profitable, you're setting yourself up for financial ruin.

Be sure to "bake" profits into your dessert menu (pardon the pun). Having a showstopper on your dessert menu that ticks all of the above boxes is a great way to win at Sale Through Service when it comes to desserts. Let's take a popular example:

Example: The House Brownie Sundae

Look – Has the table finished their mains and is ready for the next step in the guest journey?

Ask – "Who loves chocolate brownies and ice-cream?"

Propose – "Why not try our famous, hot and gooey House Brownie Sundae? Fresh daily baked house brownies, drizzled with hot fudge and caramel, layered with Cornish ice cream and topped with dark chocolate sprinkles."

So why would you recommend a dish like this to your guests?

- It's beyond delicious (that's pretty much enough of a reason for me).

- It can be quickly thrown together – but that's part of the charm. No one would go to the trouble of making this at home, I don't even own a Sundae glass!

- It can be served at speed and when you see it you know it's going straight on Instagram!

- It's a tall dessert that is a real showstopper as it gets paraded through the restaurant to its smiling (and slightly smug) recipient.

- By telling your guests it's famous, it becomes infamous – people remember it and always look for it on the menu.

- There's profit in it!

It's also ideal for when people aren't quite sure if they have enough space for a dessert – why not have one of our delicious specialities that's the perfect portion to share?

In your restaurant, you need your own show-stopping dessert that creates that wow factor and has great GP that your guests can make famous.

Time for a nightcap?

When it comes to nightcaps, it all comes down to timing. In your Pre-Service Meeting, you should establish what the goals are for tonight's service.

Is your team on a mission to elongate the time your guests will be spending with you? Or perhaps will you be on more of a turning tables mission where exceptional service at speed is more what you're aiming for? If you want to spend more time and have more opportunities to serve your guests, recommending a nightcap is a great option.

Maybe a brandy served in a warm snifter (napkin topped of course) is the perfect end to your guest's special family meal? Perhaps a Baileys on ice is the perfect end to the ladies having their monthly catch up?

Perhaps a couple of Espresso Martinis is the perfect end for the couple on their perfect first date? If your guests have time for a nightcap and you're not in a rush to seat the next booking, be sure to offer it. It can be the perfect end to what has already been an incredible night (well done!).

Sell outside the box

We have said it before, but it's so important so we shall say it again – your team must be confident to sell outside of the box.

It's the extras that we serve our guests, the premium wines, the delicious sides, the incredible desserts that not only transform our guests' experience with us but also transform our tips and our profits too.

Knowing what we have, who it is perfect for and why it is amazing can unlock our sales from fair to good and from good to great.

Remember, selling outside the box takes our guests to the front of the concert to enjoy the best dance moves Beyoncé has to offer!

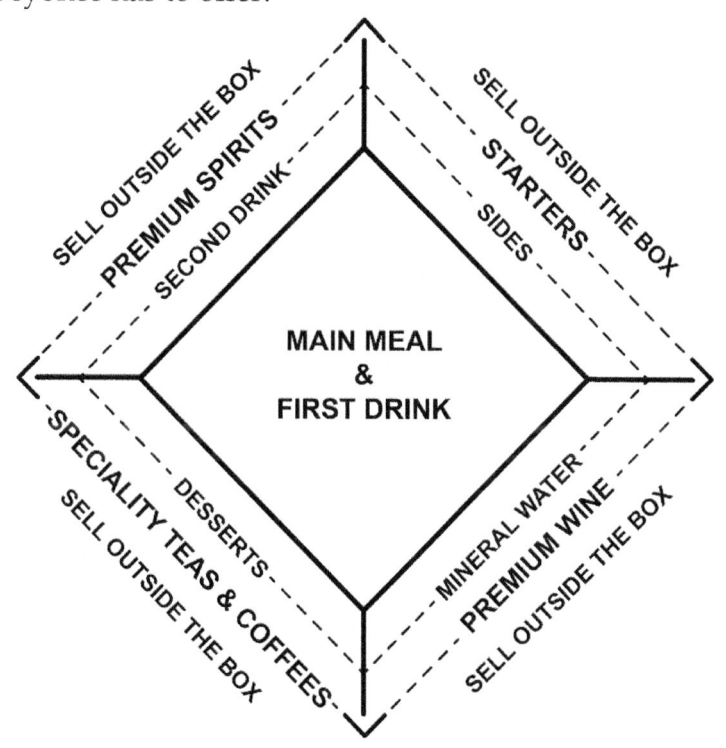

SELLING OUTSIDE THE BOX

JUST KEEP GROWING

You may have heard the saying that "data is 21st-century oil", but the reality is it's only valuable if you know what to do with it. Perhaps the saying should go "data is 21st-century *soil*". The data enables us to grow our business – if we know what to do with it.

To think our restaurants are not existing in the digital world is somewhat naive. Yes, most of our guests visit our restaurants in person, but how many of our guests scope us out online first, peruse Instagram images, check out reviews or make a booking via our website?

If we want to build on our sales success, we need to build up a system of how we can effectively capture data and, more importantly, understand what to do with it. If data is the new soil in which we *grow* our business and *nurture* our relationships, how are you planning to use this in your business?

You need to have a plan to capture your guests' data, but more importantly, you need to have a plan for what you are going to do with it. (FYI, no one cares about another newsletter, we are too busy and have too many other options trying to attract our attention).

Sales Through Social

When you have established why your guests are with you and delivered an amazing experience, what can you offer to entice them back again? Perhaps if they are premium wine drinkers, an invitation to your next wine experience night? Perhaps they are a family enjoying a special birthday – would they like to be the first to hear about your Father's Day or Christmas Day offers?

For many restaurants, knowing what to say and how to say it on social media is a struggle. It is usually left to a team member to muddle their way through and do their best. Online gurus often tell us that our social channels are not about selling but about being social, and we think with a bit of savvy strategy you can do both. For many of our restaurant's guests, the first interactions they may have with you is with the tap of a screen or seeing a share of a status update.

Because so many restaurants have asked us to solve their social media problems for them to take their business to the next level, we created Sales Through Social – giving our clients step by step content creation every single month so you never have to feel stuck on what to post. It has simplified the way our clients execute and measure their social media strategy.

Every month we guide you, complete with imagery, to give you great content plus instructions on how to grow your social accounts and, best of all, grow sales in your business. Find out more on our website: **www.thehospitalitymasters.com**

NEXT LEVEL SALES

We work with businesses of all sizes helping them to not only understand the guest journey inside their restaurant but also how to build a seamless system to have them returning again and again. So, what are some of the options to use your database for?

Key event days

Enable the people who love what you do to enjoy key events with you every single time. Your vibe is going to attract your tribe, so be sure to invite them every time there's an important event in your calendar. Burns Night, Valentines, Pancake Day, Easter, Mother's Day, Father's Day, Halloween, Christmas – if you're planning to celebrate it in style, be sure to invite your most treasured guests.

Why not create a waiting list and give away a special treat (such as a bartender's speciality cocktail) for booking in early using a special link?

Special events

Do you suffer from a summertime slump or a January sales apocalypse? Plan to buck the trend with some special events to get your raving fans back in the door.

Why not host a wine night with a special guest sommelier to walk your guests through your next season's wine list?

Even better, get your guests to pick their favourites and add those to the menu. When it comes around to peak season, where do you think your guests will be recommending to all their friends?

When the bookings diary is empty because of a particular time of year you need to think (and sell) outside the box. One of our coaching clients always suffered from a slump in sales during July and August with holidays and hen do's taking away their key demographic.

How did they compete? Well, they decided to host a special cocktail-making class from 6pm-8pm every Friday. Groups of hens and stags would descend on their bar area as a perfect start to their nights out. They not only generated extra sales through the classes, but they also had a buzzing atmosphere that attracted more guests and many of the parties would book tables to dine after the class.

Gift vouchers

Promoting gift vouchers to the guests who love what you do is a no-brainer. Dads don't want more razors or more socks! Why not promote to their grownup kids something that the whole family can benefit from – a night out at Dad's favourite restaurant with the whole family.

Christmas is the perfect time to be promoting gift vouchers, but most of our clients do a solid job of selling them all year round. How? Because they *offer* them to their guests. You can even incentivise the purchaser with a bounce-back voucher for a free appetizer or cocktail just as a thank you for them buying a voucher. This way, you won't just be welcoming back the recipient but the purchaser too. Two bookings for the price of one!

No one, and I mean no one, has the perfect business. We all need to be constantly tweaking and improving our offering, how we serve and what we sell. As we have mentioned throughout this book, it's not enough to just serve well and please our guests, hoping they will come back one day. We need a real focus on building a long lasting connection with our guests and to make an effort to invite them back to enjoy our hospitality.

TIME FOR CHANGE? TIME FOR ACTION

The reason you picked up this book is probably that you have realised something needs to change in your business. It shouldn't be such a struggle and it should be a bit more fun, right? Right. So the opportunity for change now rests on your shoulders – the question is, are you ready to lead your team?

Remember, it's not about revolution but instead embracing *evolution*. Small tweaks every day – empowering your to team to develop their knowledge, friendliness and professionalism. Your team can deliver exceptional service and sales, but they will need you to be there guiding and leading them towards success.

Be the leader that your business and your team need you to be. Stay positive and be mindful of how impactful your energy can be on others. Remember, if you make suggestions and changes in a half-hearted and inconsistent way, guess what your team will be?

Oh yes, half-hearted and inconsistent. If you set out targets but forget to check-in, give follow-up advice or reward your team, are you really fostering an environment for sales professionals to prosper? Be the leader that your business, your team members and your guests *really* need.

When it comes to recruitment, hire new starters based on attitude, not their experience.

Experience helps, but you can teach skills and they will gain experience. You can't teach having a great attitude or having a passion for people. *"Hire slow and fire fast"* has never been more relevant than when building your team of service and sales professionals.

At the beginning of this book, we looked at where you were in your business. We asked questions to understand more about what changes you would like to see and experience. Now it's time for a proposal of our own. In the Hospitality Masters, we support your business on every level. For new and existing team members, we have easy to follow, actionable training that builds confidence and habits, step by step towards being service and sales professionals.

For managers and business leaders, we have Q+As, group coaching calls, high-level how-to guides and regular support for making your business better, more profitable and operate the way it should, without you having to be there all the time.

We love being part of building up a team's expertise and getting them to feel energised about being part of a professional sales team in a restaurant. Through making small tweaks, every single day, you can without a doubt make a *huge* impact on your sales and service performance. Being part of a movement beyond your four walls can be incredibly powerful. Getting outside guidance, room to breathe and coaches on your team ready to advise and guide you to being better at what you do and how you do it.

What could happen to your business if you were to adopt the Sales Through Service system in your restaurant? What could that do for your team's spirit, your guests' experience and for your bank balance? Be curious about the effects of having a passionate and dedicated sales force. It's certainly not impossible. Trust us, we know. We help businesses like yours achieve it every day.

Don't adopt a mind-set of fear when it comes to dealing with your guests. When you look after them in a way that no one else is doing, rest assured, they will not only enjoy the experience, they will be back for more! Believe in your team's ability to follow the LAPS – to look, to ask, to propose and to serve like real professionals. With the right support from us and direction from you, the possibilities are endless.

We are not here to sell trousers or insurance policies. Instead, we are selling family time, luxury, laughter and effortlessly exceptional experiences. With your guest journey at the centre of everything you do, your sales and service levels are set for growth.

Sales Through Service is not just about reading a book and hoping your team just "get with the programme".

We have developed a system to fit into your business and to support your business and team as they grow into the sales and service professionals you so desperately want them to be. It has been designed to not only develop your team but to support you and your management team every step of the way.

Pursue progress over perfection. Yes, increasing your spend per head by £10 could be life-changing, but don't dismiss the power of £3 or £6 per head either.

Be brave, be curious, and remind your team every day…to sell really is to serve.

Visit www.thehospitalitymasters.com to find out more.

ABOUT THE AUTHORS

Deon van Niekerk

Deon van Niekerk is a London-based hospitality trainer. Since 1993, he had been working with hospitality brands to improve their businesses and, more importantly, their sales.

Having studied Marketing and Sales Management at the Technical University of Durban, South Africa he went on to work with some of London's greatest restaurants including The Ivy, Belgo, Conran Restaurants and Maxwell's Restaurant Group. He went on to found and own the critically acclaimed Cherry Jam and Neighbourhood Nightclubs in West London where service and sales were a key focus, without compromising the creative ethos of the business.

Having worked on the front line with his team, he understands first-hand why most hospitality staff hate to sell, and the difference between professional sellers and mere order takers.

Deon cofounded The Hospitality Masters, alongside Joy Zarine to assist staff in overcoming their fear of sales and helping hospitality owners and managers to set up sales systems that ensure long term success. Deon has a lifelong love of the hospitality industry and a passion for creating exceptional sales through exceptional service.

Joy Zarine

Joy Zarine is a hospitality and business strategist, industry speaker and bestselling author from London, UK. For over eighteen years, she has worked with industry leaders to create, build and market profitable and award-winning restaurants, hotels, pubs and bars.

From cocktail bartending in her teens to working and leading late night, wet-led venues in her twenties, Joy has gone on to help launch UK-wide brands and create her own hospitality and experience consultancy to develop and coach hospitality and service-based businesses.

Joy's passion lies in creating incredible customer experiences and building award-winning businesses of all sizes. She has been fortunate to work with a wide range of incredible businesses from award winning independent restaurants, to working with the world's most popular venue, The O2.

Joy is also the author of the #1 best-selling book "The Five Star Formula" in which she explains how to create incredible guest experiences that lead to five-star reviews and award-winning hospitality business.

Find out more: **www.joyzarine.com**

Printed in Great Britain
by Amazon